# The Catholic Companion to the Psalms

# The Catholic Companion to the Psalms

Mary Kathleen Glavich, SND

*acta*
PUBLICATIONS

*The Catholic Companion to the Psalms*
by Mary Kathleen Glavich, SND

Edited by Gregory F. Augustine Pierce
Cover design by Tom A. Wright
Text Design and Typesetting by Desktop Edit Shop, Inc.

Scripture quotations are from the *New Revised Standard Version Bible,* copyright © 1989 by the Division of Christian Education of the National Council of the Churches of Christ in the USA. Used by permission.

Published by ACTA Publications, 5559 W. Howard Street, Skokie, IL 60077-2621, (800) 397-2282, www.actapublications.com

Library of Congress Catalog number: 2008931390

ISBN-13: 978-0-87946-364-9

Printed in the United States of America by Evangel Press

Year 15 14 13 12 11 10 09 08
Printing 10 9 8 7 6 5 4 3 2 First

# Contents

*Dedicated to Gregory Pierce,*
*who shares my commitment*
*to spreading the faith*
*through the written word.*

# Introduction

The 150 psalms in the Bible are a precious legacy we Catholics have inherited from our spiritual ancestors. The followers of all three of the great Abrahamic religions—Jews, Christians, and Muslims—share these psalms. For three thousand years, believers throughout the world have prayed these songs of praise to express to God what was in their hearts, hoping to discover in these prayers their mysterious and longed-for God. The psalms were the daily prayer of Jesus himself, so praying them is praying the very same words the Son of God used to commune with his Father.

Countless Christians have made the psalms a part of their lives. Saints and martyrs have died with psalms on their lips: Basil the Great, Cyril of Alexandria, Francis de Sales, Francis Xavier, Teresa of Avila, Thomas à Becket, and Thomas More, to name a few. Charlemagne loved the psalms, made sure they were taught in schools, and prided himself on his nickname, David. Dorothy Day, co-founder of the Catholic Worker movement, once claimed, "My strength returns to me with my morning cup of coffee and reading the psalms." Today the Divine Office (Liturgy of the Hours), which has the psalms as its backbone, is becoming increasingly popular.

Psalms are woven through our culture and history. Great composers have set psalms and psalm verses to music, such as Handel in his stirring "Messiah." Dante sprinkled psalm verses throughout *The Divine Comedy*. At the Constitutional Convention in 1787, when the founding fathers of the United States were at an impasse in crafting the constitution, Benjamin Franklin quoted Psalm 127:1, "Unless the LORD build the house, in vain do the laborers labor" and proposed that they begin every day with prayer—inaugurating the custom that still holds in Congress. Edwin (Buzz) Aldrin, the first man to run (not walk) on the moon, on the return space flight quoted

Psalm 8:3-4: "When I consider the heavens, the work of Thy fingers, the moon and the stars, which Thou hast ordained; What is man that Thou art mindful of him?"

Like the Lord's Prayer, in fact predating it, the <u>psalms are God's response to our request,</u> "<u>Teach us to pray.</u>" Since God is the author of these prayers, along with the rest of Sacred Scripture, it's only logical (and courteous) that we pray them, because these are the words God wants to hear from us. In addition, as we pray the psalms, we accomplish the purpose for which we were created: to praise and love God, our Creator.

Despite this widespread use and unparalleled origin—and although a "psalms" search on the Internet brings up more than two million results—for too many Catholics the psalms remain an unopened gift, an undiscovered treasure, with the possible exceptions of Psalm 23, the Good Shepherd psalm, and the responsorial psalms at Mass. Many people are unaware of how perfectly the psalms resonate with the deep feelings of all human beings, including their own.

On the other hand, some people who do pray the psalms—even daily as I do—glide over the familiar words, often oblivious to their meanings, both literal and symbolic. We may even often find our minds drifting elsewhere. The psalms ordinarily do not leap off the page, grab us, and shake us up as they have the potential to do as God's living word.

*The Catholic Companion to the Psalms* is a treasury of methods for understanding and praying the psalms. Although it is not a commentary on individual psalms, its bibliography suggests sources that serve that purpose. May this book be the catalyst that brings the psalms to life for all seekers and pray-ers. May it entice all of us to begin or continue to mine the riches of these simple but powerful prayers and use them for ardent heart-to-heart conversations with God. And may we all be in tune with Saint Augustine, who claimed, "My Psalter is my joy."

# Prelude
# A Bit of Background

*"Praise the LORD!"*
Psalm 106:1

his chapter might hold more than you need or want to know in order to pray the psalms. Feel free to skip it. If you're interested in the psalms, however, you will find the information here fascinating. It is presented in the form of frequently asked questions and answers for easier reading.

## What is a psalm?

A psalm is a Jewish hymn or lyrical poem in praise of God. The word *psalm* comes from the Greek *psalmos*, which means "a song sung to a plucked instrument." The Jews call the psalms *Tehillim*, which in English is "songs of praise." So psalms are God-centered. F. Vigouroux, S.S., observed that all but seventeen psalms name God in the very first verse. To Christians, psalms are also Christ-centered; for Christ is God, he prayed the psalms, and the psalms prophesy his coming and many aspects of his life.

The psalms are not intended to be theological or historical writing. They are first and foremost prayers. The human attitudes and sentiments—often raw emotions—that they express strike a chord in the hearts of people of all generations. Moreover, the psalms show that all the stuff of our everyday lives is material for prayer and dialogue with our ever-present God.

♪ psalm notes…

For a quiz on the Book of Psalms, log onto www.quiz. christiansunite.com/ The_Book_of_Psalms/.

## What is the Book of Psalms?

If a psalm is a song of praise, the Book of Psalms is a symphony of praise. The Old Testament is divided into three sections: the Torah, the Prophetic books, and the Writings. The Book of Psalms, the longest book in the Bible, belongs to the Writings and is considered one of the wisdom books. The psalms were composed by the Hebrew people over a span of at least 600 years, from about 1500 B.C. to 430 B.C. as God gradually revealed himself to them. The Book of Psalms, also called the Psalter, is a collection of individual collections of various psalms. That is why some of the psalms repeat. (Psalm 14 and 53 are identical. Psalm 40:13–17 is the entire Psalm 70. Psalm 108 is a combination of Psalm 57:7–11 and Psalm 60:5–12). The Psalter was compiled in its current form by the third century B.C.

The Book of Psalms is the prayer book of the Old Testament and the prayer book of Israel. It is also called the hymn book of the Second Temple, which was dedicated in 515 B.C., because many of the psalms were prayed there. It is said that if the whole Old Testament were lost except for Psalms, we would still know all the Old Testament concepts because Psalms is a microcosm of its other books. Creation, the history of Israel, wisdom, prophecies, and attitudes toward life and suffering—all are echoed in the psalms. In addition, because the psalms point to the Messiah described in the New Testament, Martin Luther correctly called the Psalter "the Bible in miniature." Today we might say the psalms are the Cliff Notes of the Bible.

## Who composed the psalms?

Most people assume that the author of the psalms is Israel's King David, someone the prophet Samuel

10

once described as a man after the Lord's own heart. Actually no one knows who the human writers of the psalms were. Existing first as oral prayers, the songs survived in Hebrew worship and were written down only later. The oldest psalms are modeled on and even partly lifted from Canaanite hymns to pagan gods. Psalm 103 closely resembles a song to Aton, the Egyptian sun-god from the time of Akhnaton. Some psalms date back to times before David, while many of them refer to events after his era, such as the exile in Babylon. Nevertheless, traditionally the psalms are called the songs of David. Why? As a boy, David soothed King Saul by playing the lyre. According to Sirach 47:8–10, King David "sang praise with all his heart" and "placed singers before the altar" to add beauty to the festivals so that "the sanctuary resounded from early morning." Besides, King David was a great hero, and people tend to give writings credibility by attributing them to esteemed public figures, a tradition accepted by the unknown author of this ditty:

*King David and King Solomon*
*Led merry, merry lives*
*With many, many lady friends*
*And many, many wives!*
*But when their lives were ending,*
*Both were seized with qualms.*
*So Solomon wrote the Proverbs*
*And David wrote the Psalms!*

♪ psalm notes...

Psalm 29, the oldest psalm, probably originated as a psalm to Baal, the Canaanite storm god. It is called the "the seven-thunder psalm" because of the repetition of "The voice of the LORD." The psalm powerfully describes a storm moving from the Mediterranean Sea to Lebanon and on to the distant land of Kadesh.

### How do the psalms of the Hebrews differ from the prayer-songs of their contemporaries?

The psalms are directed to Yahweh, the supreme, all-powerful God, who is distinct from the things he created. The pagan gods, on the other hand, were identified with the sun, the moon, the stars,

The Lutheran theologian Dietrich Bonhoeffer wrote in his book *Psalms: The Prayer Book of the Bible*, "Whenever the Psalter is abandoned, an incomparable treasure vanishes from the Christian church. With its recovery will come unsuspected power."

and other created things. Yahweh is good and just, whereas the pagan gods displayed the same faults as creatures. Most significantly, Yahweh is not only in the heavens but also quite near, in fact, dwelling with the Hebrews themselves. The God of Israel is a very personal God who cares for his people like a mother or father. This is a far cry from most of the pagan gods, who were cold, silent, and distant from human beings and sometimes had to be placated by the sacrifice of human lives on the altars of their creatures.

## When were the psalms sung?

The Hebrew people sang the psalms both alone as part of their daily prayer and with the community. Parents sang psalms to their children to instruct them in the loving and saving ways of God and how to act as a member of God's people. The psalms were sung by a group during liturgies and sacrifices at the Temple in Jerusalem, during festivals, and as pilgrimage songs on the way to the Temple. They also figured in the services at local synagogues, such as the one Jesus, Mary and Joseph would have attended in Nazareth.

## How were the psalms sung?

Singing a psalm in a Temple liturgy was a grand production, apparently comparable to a Christian rock concert today. The Israelites sang psalms exuberantly and loudly with cries, shouts, moans, and joyful exclamations as well as with handclapping, dancing, lifting of hands, prostrations, low bows, and kneeling with the forehead touching the ground in the manner of Muslim prayer today.

The structure of the psalms indicate that they were sung in a variety of ways. For example, a leader might alternate with all the people, or a chorus might alternate with soloists. The Temple had a chorus of professional singers from a Levitical (priestly) family. According to Mishnah (Jewish writings), these were twelve male singers. Biblical scholars propose that after a singer asked God for something on behalf of a petitioner, a priest would assure the petitioner of God's answer, and the singer would then express thanksgiving—all by using the psalms. Psalms that we recite or sing today in a minute or so could extend for two hours in the Temple because of the petitions, musical interludes, and repetitions.

## What instruments were played with the psalms?

The singing of psalms was accompanied by many instruments. Psalm 150 names trumpet, lute, harp, tambourine, strings, pipe, and clanging, clashing cymbals. There were also the shofar (a ram's horn), a bell, and a small drum. Unfortunately, the original melodies of the psalms have vanished in the dust of the ages, as elusive as the proverbial lost chord.

## Who is speaking in the psalms?

Usually either an individual or the whole community is speaking in the psalms. Sometimes, though, as in Psalm 118, one person speaks in the name of the entire community, using the first-person singular. God speaks in only five psalms (Psalms 50, 75, 81, 87, and 95). Some psalms, such as Psalms 49, 74, and 84, contain prophecies, which may have been pronounced by a Temple priest.

♪ psalm notes...

Saint Thomas Aquinas viewed the psalms as three groups of fifty, reflecting the three states of the faithful: the state of penitence in the first fifty (which in his Bible concluded with Psalm 51: "Have mercy on my, O God" Psalm 51:1); the state of justice and being judged in the second fifty (which ends with "I will sing of loyalty and of justice" Psalm 101:1); and the state of praising eternal glory in the third fifty (which concludes "Let everything that breathes praise the LORD!" Psalm 150:6).

13

A Hebrew shield was five-feet high and protected the entire body. When a psalm calls God my "shield," it implies that God is caring for my whole being.

## How are the psalms organized?

The psalms are grouped into five sections of unequal length, each a medley of themes. Some suppose that this division is modeled on the Jewish Torah or Pentateuch, the first five books of the Bible, which contain God's direct teachings. Each section ends with a doxology (a short prayer of praise) that has been appended to the last psalm in that section. The five sections and their doxologies are:

❖ Psalms 1–41 (41:14)
❖ Psalms 42–72 (72:18)
❖ Psalms 73–89 (89:53)
❖ Psalms 90–106 (106:48)
❖ Psalms 107–150 (150).

Psalm 1 and Psalm 150 are like bookends for the Psalter. Psalm 1 is really not a psalm or a prayer. It is a beatitude (that is, it begins "Happy are those...") and a statement about God's law and the benefit of living by it. Psalm 2 is a hymn about God's kingdom. So from the outset, the Book of Psalms focuses on the law and the kingdom. Psalms 1 and 2 serve as an overture for the rest of the book. The grand finale of this book of praise is Psalm 150, a magnificent doxology and the only praise psalm that doesn't give a reason to praise. It crescendos until its last words exclaim, "Let everything that breathes praise the LORD! Praise the LORD," making it a fitting conclusion to this book of praise.

## What does the word *selah* in the margin of some psalms mean?

Although the word *selah* appears 71 times, punctuating 39 psalms, this word baffles scholars. Proposed explanations of what *selah* signals include a musical interlude, a blast of loud music, a refrain, praying louder, or kneeling, bowing, or prostrating. *Selah* might also indicate "Stop and think."

## Why are there different versions of the psalms?

Some translations of the Bible are based on the original Hebrew Bible (Masoretic text), while others are based on the Greek Bible (the Septuagint) that originated later in Alexandria, Egypt. Saint Jerome wrote three translations of the psalms. His translation of Origin's Greek psalms (Hexapla) into Latin around 386-391 A.D. was included in his Latin Bible (the Vulgate). This version, known as the Gallican Psalter, was the basis of Gregorian chant. It was the official translation for liturgy in the West beginning with the time of Charlemagne until 2000, when the New Vulgate translation based on the Masoretic text replaced it. The psalms have also been rewritten many times in language that speaks more to modern people. See the Bibliography for some versions of the psalms available today.

## Why do the numbers of the psalms differ in some Bibles?

The Hebrew Scriptures are often one digit ahead of the Greek and Latin Bibles, which join Psalms 9 and 10 as well as 114 and 115 but divide both 116 and 147 into two parts. Newer versions of the Bible are based on the Hebrew Scriptures.

## Why does the numbering of psalm verses differ in some Bibles?

Some Bibles identify a psalm's introductory information as verse 1, while others begin numbering with the psalm itself.

♪ psalm notes...

In Psalm 16:7, "my heart instructs me," the Hebrew is actually "kidneys," not "heart," because the kidneys were considered vital and signified the essence of a person.

## Information Provided by Superscriptions

Most psalms have introductory lines, or "superscriptions," many of them technical directions for the leader or choirmaster. These often begin, "To the leader." The thirty-four psalms that have no headings are dubbed "orphan psalms." The superscriptions were added during a later editing of the Book of Psalms. Their meanings are often a mystery, but because they are so old they are traditionally included in most Bibles. These labels serve several purposes:

❖ **The "author."** Most psalms are attributed to David (73 psalms). It's not known whether the psalm headings that refer to David mean that the psalm is by him, for him, authorized by him, or written during his reign, during his dynasty, or in the manner of David. Other psalms are attributed to Solomon (2), Asaph (12), Korah (12), Heman (1), Ethan (1), and Moses (1). Solomon was David's son and successor. Asaph was a leader of David's Levite (priestly) choir who had many descendants. Korah (or Korahim) refers to a guild of Temple singers or musicians. Fifty psalms are not ascribed to anyone.

❖ **Occasion in David's life.** Some psalms are associated with a time in David's life. For example, the penitential Psalm 51 is headed "when the prophet Nathan came to him, after he had gone in to Bathsheba."

❖ **Instrumentation**. The musical instruments required are sometimes stated, such as stringed or wind instruments.

❖ **Melody**. Some headings include "according to," which is thought to mean "to the tune of." For example, Psalm 45 is to be played "according to Lilies," where Lilies is presumed to be a song.

❖ **Juduthan**. Psalms 39, 62, and 77 refer to Jeduthan, who was a Temple musician.

❖ **Type of song**. Fifty-seven psalms are labeled *mizmor* or "psalm," meaning accompanied by a string instrument; and twelve psalms are labeled "song." Some headings tell the type of poem the psalm is. Thirteen psalms are labeled *maskil*, which is thought to indicate a reflective or didactic psalm. Scholars can only guess at the meaning of *miktam*, which occurs before six psalms.

❖ **When to pray**. For some psalms an appropriate time to pray them is noted, such as on the Sabbath or when one is thankful or afflicted. Those described as "a song of ascent" were probably sung on the way to Jerusalem to pray at the Temple there.

## Are there psalms other than those in the Book of Psalms?

We know that other collections of psalms existed that were not included in the Bible. There are also psalms in other books of the Old Testament. Miriam's song after the Hebrews passed safely through the Reed Sea is one. Jonah's prayer in the belly of the large fish is another. The lovely prayer of Habakkuk in Habakkuk 3 is thought to have been a psalm added to this prophet's book. Likewise, the New Testament contains psalms. Three Christian psalms that the Church prays everyday in the Divine Office are Zechariah's song at the circumcision of his son, John the Baptist (*"Benedictus"*), Mary's canticle when she visits Elizabeth (*"Magnificat"*), and Simeon's song on beholding the Savior (*"Nunc Dimittis"*). Certain passages in the New Testament letters are clearly early Christians hymns, such as Colossians 1:15–20.

An additional psalm, Psalm 151, attributed to David appears in the original Hebrew text and in the Dead Sea Scroll of psalms, though it is regarded as apocryphal. Its seven verses recount how David was chosen and anointed instead of his older brothers and how he played psalms and slew a giant idol-worshipper to remove reproach from Israel.

## What is the oldest known copy of the Psalms in existence?

The Dead Sea Scrolls, discovered in eleven caves in Qumran on the West Bank from 1947 to 1956, contain 36 copies of Psalms. In 1956, a manuscript of psalms and hymns dating from 30 to 50 A.D. was found in Cave 11. Among them were parts of forty-one biblical psalms. The scroll, probably calf-

♪ psalm notes...

The Psalms of Solomon is a collection of eighteen psalms probably written about the first or second century B.C. Early Christian writers referred to it, but no copy existed until a Greek translation was discovered in the seventeenth century.

In Psalm 51:1, "Have mercy on me, O God," the Hebrew word for "mercy" used here is derived from the word for "womb," indicating that we are asking God to show mother-love toward us.

skin, contains 28 columns of carefully written script. Six or seven lines are missing at the bottom of each. The Dead Sea Scrolls are housed in Jerusalem in a museum called the Shrine of the Book. The dome of the building is shaped like the top of one of the clay jars in which many of the scrolls were found.

# God the Lyricist

*"Your word is a lamp to my feet."*
Psalm 119:105

In a class for lectors (readers at liturgy) a young man got up and read aloud Psalm 23, which begins, "The LORD is my shepherd." When he finished, the class applauded politely. Then an elderly gentleman stood and read the same psalm. At the end, there was complete silence—everyone was so moved by his rendition. The spell was broken when the young man wisely commented, "I know Psalm 23, but he knows the Good Shepherd."

This story reinforces the truth that the psalms are intimately connected with God. In fact, the psalms are God's words, which he inspired people to write. Like the other books in Scripture, the Book of Psalms is "the word of God in the words of human beings." What does this mean?

## The Power of God's Word

At the dawn of creation God's word was at work. According to Genesis, the first book of the Bible, to orchestrate the formation of the cosmos, God simply spoke. At his word, out of chaos came order and beauty. First God said, "Let there be light," and there was light. Then at God's subsequent commands an astonishing array of creatures appeared. The millions of twinkling stars in the sky, our jewel of a planet Earth, immense oceans, jagged snow-capped mountains, as well as the trees and flowers growing in your own backyard—all are the result of God's word. Most awesome of all, God's word summoned us human beings into existence. It is not just a coincidence that in Hebrew the word for "speak," *dabar*, is also the word for "create."

19

Psalm 117, the short-
est psalm with only
two verses, is the
center chapter of the
Bible's 1,189 chapters.
The middle line of this
psalm is "For great is
his steadfast love to-
ward us." Coinciden-
tally this is the main
theme that runs
through the entire
Bible.

God's word pre-existed creation. The opening verses of John's Gospel relate this everlasting Word to creation: "In the beginning was the Word, and the Word was with God, and the Word was God. He was in the beginning with God. All things came into being through him, and without him not one thing came into being" (John 1:1-3).

Theologians try to explain the unexplainable, the mystery of the Trinity. They say that the Son is "begotten by" and "proceeds from" the Father as an act of the divine mind from all eternity. Similar to the way our thoughts are expressed in words, the Father's reflections about himself are expressed as Word. But because God is so great, his Word, unlike ours, is a Person equal in divinity. This Second Person constantly praises, that is, acknowledges the perfections of the First Person. It could be said that the Son is always psalming the Father.

That Word of God "became flesh and lived among us." We Catholics believe that Jesus was God, and therefore his utterances were the word of God. What happened when Jesus spoke? Incredibly, the blind could see, the deaf could hear, lepers were healed, sinners were forgiven, and the searching learned the true meaning of life. When Jesus spoke, roaring winds and towering waves died down, plain water became the best wine, and bread and fish multiplied. At Jesus' word, even a man who had been dead for four days walked out of his tomb. A Roman centurion realized the amazing potency of Jesus' word. When his servant was sick, this man of faith pleaded with Jesus, "Only speak the word, and my servant will be healed" (Matthew 8:8).

### God Present in Scripture

Here's an awesome but true thought: We come into contact with this same almighty word whenever we read the words of Scripture or hear them pro-claimed—and whenever we pray the psalms. Saint Augustine recommended that we place ourselves before the Scriptures as though we were before the face of God. God is mysteriously present, living and breathing in the Bible, including the psalms. Every contact with Scripture is an opportunity for a God-encounter that could be life-changing.

In his book *With Hearts Burning,* Henri Nouwen explains how Scripture operates. He points out that (like the seven sacraments) the word of God makes present what it indicates. In fact, the Bible is the greatest of all the "sacramentals." Merely hearing God's word can change us. Nouwen recalls the two dejected disciples who were on the way to Emmaus after the crucifixion. They had lost all hope until a stranger (who was really the risen Lord) joined them. When Jesus was interpreting the Scripture for them, the disciples' hearts burned within them. They experienced the Lord's real presence in the words of Scripture (Luke 24:13-32).

Likewise for us, the full power of the word does not largely lie in how we apply it after we have heard it. The transforming power of the word does its divine work as we listen. When we listen well, then our hearts too will burn within us, for we are in the presence of Jesus. The prophet Isaiah de-scribes the effectiveness of the divine word:

*For as the rain and the snow come down from heaven,*
*and do not return there*
*until they have watered the earth,*
*making it bring forth and sprout,*
*giving seed to the sower and bread to the eater,*
*so shall my word be that goes out from my mouth:*
*it shall not return to me empty,*
*but it shall accomplish that which I purpose,*
*and succeed in the thing for which I sent it.*

Isaiah 55:10-11

♪ psalm notes...

The psalms are in the Jewish prayer book (*Siddur*). In times of trouble Jews pray the psalms and might even divide them among the members of the community so all of them are prayed.

As an integral part of Scripture, the psalms, simple yet dynamic prayers, bring us into the presence, peace, and power of God. They have power to heal, change, guide, comfort, and give life. As one saint put it, "Scripture tills the soil of your soul." With such tilling, God's life can grow and bear fruit in us.

## God's Living Word

Have you ever had the startling but pleasant experience of reading or listening to a familiar passage of the Bible and suddenly the words electrify you? They speak directly to a situation you are in. If so, you know then the truth of what God told Jeremiah: "Is not my word like fire…like a hammer that breaks a rock in pieces?" (Jeremiah 23:29) Scripture says about itself, "The word of God is living and active, sharper than any two-edged sword" (Hebrews 4:12).

The Bible was written thousands of years ago for a people whose culture was totally different from ours. We do not deal with camels, tents, animal sacrifices, and spear-and-arrow battles, but with cars, condominiums, computers, cell phones, and the threat of nuclear war. How can this ancient book possibly have meaning for us? The answer is that the Bible is a classic. Like Shakespeare's plays and Dickens' novels, Scripture revolves around basic ageless questions that people continue to grapple with: Who am I? Who is God? What is God like? Why do we suffer? What is death? What is love?

An artist named Kathe Kollwitz, who lived in Nazi Germany, drew a picture of a haggard adult embracing and sheltering some wide-eyed children. After losing two sons in World War I, Kathe created this piece of art as a warning against launching another world war. She titled her work "The Seed Corn Must Not Be Sown." Seed corn is the portion

## God's Love Songs

Here are a few psalm verses that show God as a tremendous lover who is both seductive and tender.

"You have made them [human beings] a little lower than God, and crowned them with glory and honor." (Psalm 8:5)

"If my father and mother forsake me, the LORD will take me up." (Psalm 27:10)

"Steadfast love surrounds those who trust in the LORD." (Psalm 32:10)

"The LORD holds us by the hand." (Psalm 37:24)

"You have multiplied, O LORD my God, your wondrous deeds and your thoughts toward us." (Psalm 40:5)

"He will be our guide forever." (Psalm 48:14)

"But you, O LORD, are a God merciful and gracious, slow to anger and abounding in steadfast love and faithfulness." (Psalm 86:15)

"When they call to me, I will answer them; I will be with them in trouble, I will rescue them and honor them." (Psalm 91:15)

"As a father has compassion for his children, so the LORD has compassion for those who fear him." (Psalm 103:13)

"He who keeps you will not slumber." (Psalm 121:3)

"If I take the wings of the morning and settle at the farthest limits of the sea, even there your hand shall lead me, and your right hand shall hold me fast." (Psalm 139:9–10)

of seed that farmers do not plant but store away for the following year in case the crops should fail. Kathe's picture was a plea not to wipe out future generations. Looking at her illustration today, people might not know the story behind it. Nevertheless using the context of their life, they can extract their own meaning from this powerful picture. In a world that regularly sees abortion, abused children, homelessness, epidemics, and refugees, they discover that this drawing still speaks to them.

Like meaning in art, the meaning of God's word is not frozen but living. It is always fresh and new, multi-layered like Russian nesting dolls. People coming to Scripture from their individual perspectives continue to interact with its messages from generation to generation. The Spirit alive in our hearts helps us listen to God's word. The Spirit alive in the community of the Church speaks directly to us in our technological age as we face new issues of life and death, right and wrong. Because of the Spirit's action, we are able to "actualize" the word, that is, to understand its meaning in light of the circumstances of our lives.

In the rhythm of the psalms we hear the heartbeat of God. Someone has called the Bible a book drenched in love. God gave us words to praise him in the psalms, and they are clearly God's love songs. They reveal God's passionate, unconditional love for us, his people. The psalms mention God's *hesed*, translated "steadfast love," some 96 times. Someone pointed out that in Scripture not only do we search for God, but God searches for us.

# Psalm Modes

*"To you, O LORD, I lift up my soul."*
Psalm 25:1

Songs come in different forms and styles, each with particular characteristics. Consider the variety: operatic arias, national anthems, camp songs, and nursery rhymes. Then there are symphonies, blues, country, rock-and-roll, and rap. It's no surprise, then, that the hymns in the Book of Psalms are of different genres. They are appropriate for the ups and downs and in-betweens of our roller-coaster life, as the following story demonstrates.

One woman was captured and sold into sexual slavery. She was beaten, raped, and tortured repeatedly. Eventually a team from International Justice Mission rescued her. They found she had written these words on the wall of the room where she had been held: "The LORD is my light and my salvation; whom shall I fear? The LORD is the stronghold of my life; of whom shall I be afraid? When evildoers assail me to devour my flesh—my adversaries and foes—they shall stumble and fall. Though an army encamp against me, my heart shall not fear; though war rise up against me, yet I will be confident" (Psalm 27:1-3). After she was rescued, people asked her to read these psalm verses for them, but she replied, "No. Those were the words I prayed when I was in the brothel. But I will read you these words: 'I will bless the LORD at all times; his praise shall continually be in my mouth. My soul makes its boast in the LORD; let the humble hear and be glad. O magnify the LORD with me; and let us exalt his name together. I sought the LORD, and he answered me, and delivered me from all my fears'" (Psalm 34:1-4).

The German scholar Hermann Gunkel (1863–1932) was the first to categorize psalms based on their life-setting, purpose, and structure. The Nor-

Although the psalms may be considered foreign and/or primitive to us, the Book of Psalms is a school of prayer. Reading it, we learn different ways to approach God. We can speak to God in the words of the psalms themselves— or in our own words that are modeled on the psalms—whenever we are glad, sad, mad, or have been bad.

wegian Sigmund Wowinckel and others like Claus Westermann have modified his classifications and made new proposals regarding how the psalms were used originally. Nevertheless, attempts to neatly classify the psalms are in vain because often they are a medley of themes. The following are the usual ways the psalms are grouped, along with occasions when you might wish to pray them.

## Laments: The Blues in the Bible

Most of the psalms (at least forty) are *laments*, in which an individual or the people as a whole are acknowledging their total dependence on God, complaining to him, and declaring their trust in his help. These elements reflect Israel's history, which, according to Walter Brueggemann, "is shaped and interpreted as an experience of cry and rescue." The reasons for the laments vary: sickness, sin, old age, unjust accusation, or enemies. Most laments in midstream do a U-turn, however, and the complaining changes to thanks and praise (except for Psalm 88, which is totally dark). The basic structure of laments makes them easily recognizable. A lament usually begins with a cry to God, such as "O God" or "O LORD." This is followed by a complaint, a declaration of trust (often based on what God did in the past), a petition, an assurance (probably by a priest) that God will hear the prayer, and a vow to praise God or offer sacrifice. Lament psalms are Psalms 3, 4, 5, 6, 7, 13, 17, 22a, 27, 28, 31, 35, 38, 41, 42, 43, 51, 54, 55, 56, 57, 59, 60, 61, 64, 69, 70, 71, 74, 77, 79, 80, 83, 86, 88, 90, 94, 102, 109, 120, 130, 137, 140, 141, 142, 143.

Saint Ambrose called the psalms "the gymnasium of the soul." Through the laments, we are able to work through feelings of rage and frustration. We can pray these pleading psalms whenever we're trapped in a crisis or life has dealt us a blow. If our pain is excruciating, it helps to pray a lament boldly with a strong voice, even shouting. Like the Israelites, we should be confident that our good and loving God will hear our petition. In his book *Sacred Sorrow,* author Michael Card laments the fact that contemporary worship does not employ prayers of lament! He views the lament psalms as an honest, mature way to pray our fears, doubts, anger, and disappointments.

Psalm 77 is a good lament to pray when we are in trouble or faced with a problem. How easy it is to identify with the psalmist who seeks God's help but isn't comforted. He doesn't sleep at night. He can't talk. He wonders if God has stopped loving him. But then the psalmist remembers how God led the people on a perilous walk through the Reed Sea, amid lightning and earthshaking thunder. Though the mountains of water were piled up on either side of them, ready to crash down, the Israelites came through safely. We need to ride out the storm, trusting in God's providence to bring about good.

## Praise Psalms

The second largest group of psalms is *praise* psalms in which the psalmist acknowledges and marvels at God's perfections and creations and bursts forth in exultation. Praise is our fundamental response to God simply because of who God is. We are in awe of the Holy One whose wisdom and power designed the 1.8 million species cataloged so far and the numberless stars and planets swirling through space, trillions of miles from us. We are astonished at this God whose love called us into being and whose mercy led the Word to became one of us in order to save us and show us the way. In such moments when we are aware of God's infinite majesty and goodness that it takes our breath away, what else can we do but praise him?

Most of us are inclined to associate praying with asking for things. In reality, praise is the first and foremost prayer. Moreover, in the next world, there will be no need for prayers of petition, but giving glory to God will not only endure but will become our "full-time" occupation.

Praise psalms usually open with a call to praise, state the reason to praise (e.g., creation or deliverance), and then repeat the introduction or give a blessing. There are two kinds of praise psalms. *Narrative* praise psalms recount God's saving acts, while *descriptive* praise psalms proclaim God's attributes such as his power, goodness, or fidelity. Some praise psalms—namely Psalms 8, 19, 65, 104, and 148—are also referred to as creation psalms because they praise God as creator, harking back to Genesis. They incorporate nature, as do pagan prayers. But to the Hebrews, their God transcended the sun, the moon, and all other created things that their neighbors worshiped as gods.

One set of praise psalms is the Egyptian Hallel (praise) psalms (Psalms 113–118), which are sung after the Passover meal. They are so-named because of Psalm 114:1—"When Israel went out from Egypt." Most of the Hallel psalms end with *Hallelujah* (our present-day *alleluia*). This acclamation means "Praise the Lord," for it is composed of the Hebrew word *hallel* (praise) combined with the first syllable of *Yahweh*. Another set of praise psalms is the five last psalms, Psalms 146–150. These all begin and end with *Hallelujah*. Other praise psalms are Psalms 29, 33, 68, 100, 103, 105, 111, 134, 135, and 139.

Times we might pray a praise psalm include when we are caught up by the beauty and intricate mysteries of nature, when we have experienced an extraordinary (or ordinary) blessing, or when we look back on our lives and recognize God's loving hand at work. Praise psalms help give voice to our thoughts and feelings of awe, reverence, love of the Lord, and joy.

One favorite psalm is Psalm 100 or, as it's fondly called, "Old Hundredth." It is the basis of the stately hymn "Praise God from Whom All Blessings Flow" and innumerable other versions titled "Jubilate Deo." A gem of a praise psalm that sparkles with energy and enthusiasm for the Lord, Psalm 100 is fitting to pray at times when we are so overwhelmed by God's holiness and goodness that we can hardly contain ourselves. In this psalm we call on all the earth to make a joyful noise in worship of God. We reflect on the tremendous and consoling truth that God made us and we belong to him. Again we call on all peoples to come into God's presence and thank, praise, and bless him. Why? Because the Lord is good and his steadfast love is forever.

## Thanksgiving Psalms

There are also psalms of *thanksgiving*: Psalms 9, 18, 30, 34, 41, 66, 92, 103, 107, 116, 118, 124 , 136, 138, which are similar to psalms of praise because the Hebrews had no separate word for or concept of thanks. *Tohar* meant both praise and thanks. In fact, instead of expressing thanks to a person in return for a gift or favor, the Israelites pronounced a blessing, believing that they conferred strength, life, and prosperity through their words. When the Israelites "blessed" God, they were acknowledging that God is full of blessing and the source and giver of all blessings. In effect, they were praising God and proclaiming what God has done.

Thanksgiving psalms are a response to obtaining

♪ psalm notes...

Some psalms are anthological (a word meaning "collection of flowers"), that is, they incorporate lines from other books in the Bible and from other psalms. In Psalm 1, for instance, the comparison of a good person to a fruitful tree near water echoes Jeremiah 1:7–8. Psalm 18 is also found in 2 Samuel 22. Psalm 86 is a patchwork of about forty tidbits from other psalms and from the Torah.

The superscription for Psalm 92 reads, "A Song for the Sabbath Day." One Jewish tradition is that Adam composed this psalm for the first Sabbath.

a request. It seems that the Israelites prayed them on the occasions when they were making thanksgiving sacrifice. Scholars venture to say that Psalm 107 was prayed as successive groups offered thanksgiving sacrifices: travelers (verses 4–9), prisoners (verses 10–16), the sick (verses 17–22), and sailors (verses 23–32). Naturally, we would most likely turn to a thanksgiving psalm when we receive the answer to a prayer or when God sends us an unexpected gift or grace.

## Minor Categories

The *historical* psalms offer an overview of the wonderful saving deeds God has accomplished for Israel, especially bringing them from slavery to the promised land through the Exodus, which is the subject of twenty psalms. Some salvation history psalms are Psalms 78, 105, 106, 135, and 136. For both the Israelites and us, remembering makes the historical happening present again. (This is true, for example, whenever we Catholics celebrate Mass.) Our God is a living God who is always loving and saving us. We can pray the historical psalms to renew our faith in God's actions of the past as well as of the present. The redemption cycle played out in the Old Testament with Moses and the chosen people was repeated in the New Testament with Christ and his Church and continues today.

In the seven *penitential* psalms the contrite prayer asks forgiveness for sins. They are Psalms 6, 32, 38, 51, 102, 130, and 143. Obviously, we would pray the penitential psalms when we realize that we (our family, our nation) have sinned and are sorry. They are especially appropriate when celebrating the sacrament of reconciliation and during the season of Lent, when we repent of our sins and resolve once again to live the Gospel.

Psalms of *confidence* or *trust* in our good and loving God are Psalms 4, 11, 16, 23, 46, 62, 63, 90, 91, 115, 121, 125, and 131. These psalms are fitting at times when trouble, insecurity, anxiety, or depression plagues us. Their words bring consolation and comfort and renew our hope. For this reason, they are often prayed at the bedsides of the sick and dying.

The *wisdom* or didactic psalms are instructive and reflective. Like the proverbs, many of them point out the right path that is followed by those who will be blessed. They are Psalms 1, 18, 32, 34, 37, 49, 73, 112, 119, 127, 128, and 138. In times of temptation, these psalms can motivate us to stay close to God and follow the Way.

Psalms of *enthronement* celebrate the Lord's kingship over Israel, all nations, and the whole world. They are Psalms 47, 93, 95, 96, 97, 98, 99, and 100. Wowinckel proposed that these were sung at an annual enthronement ritual at the Temple. They declare, "Yahweh reigns," which is what all of creation attests to as it manifests his glory. Some of these psalms look to the Lord's coming, when he will establish his kingdom of justice. Like the praise psalms, enthronement psalms can be prayed when we are filled with awe at God and God's deeds.

Another category of psalms are *royal* psalms about the king. Psalm 18 gives thanks for the king; Psalms 20 and 144:1–11 are a plea for the king's safety; Psalm 21 thanks for blessings on the king; Psalm 45 is a song for a royal wedding; and Psalms 2, 72, 110, and 101 have to do with the king's style of ruling. A subcategory of royal psalms are the *messianic* psalms about the future king. They are Psalms 2, 15, 21, 44, 71, and 109. Even when the Jews no longer had a king, they prayed the royal psalms in view of their expecting the king of kings, the Messiah. Christians pray these psalms as referring in

♪ psalm notes...

Saint Augustine was a sinner who became a Christian, a bishop, and a saint. His autobiography is the well-known *Confessions*. When Augustine was dying, he had the seven penitential psalms written on the wall of his room so he could pray them.

A copy of Psalm 8 is on the moon. In 1969 Neil Armstrong and Buzz Aldrin left a silicon disk on the moon containing messages from the leaders of seventy-two countries, including Pope Paul VI, who quoted Psalm 8.

### A New Means of Classification

More recently, eminent Old Testament scholar Walter Brueggemann, using the psychological concepts of Paul Ricoeur, labeled the psalms as *psalms of orientation* (a time of status quo and security, everything going on as normal), *psalms of disorientation* (a time of crisis when everything runs amok, a chance for growth), and *psalms of reorientation* (when the crisis is resolved, a new level of being exists, and thanks is rendered to God). These three stages are in sync with the rhythms of human life. Reflect on your own life's journey. Some days everything is calm. Suddenly you are confronted with a major decision or a problem that causes stress: a move, a broken relationship, a career change. Sooner or later the matter is resolved and you experience gratitude, triumph, and joy. Bruggemann uses Philippians 2:5–11 to illustrate this movement in Christ's life:

Orientation: "Though he was in the form of God...."
Disorientation: "He emptied himself."
Reorientation: "Therefore God has highly exalted him...."

Which of these three stages of life are you currently in? You might pray the type of psalms that correspond to how you feel.

their fullest sense to Jesus Christ. We can pray the royal psalms for our own government leaders, and they are also suitable for all the feasts of Christ.

Psalms of *Zion* or *Sion* (Jerusalem), the glorious holy city where God dwelt in a special way, are Psalms 46, 48, 74, 76, 84, 87, 122, and 132. These psalms can be prayed thinking of heaven, which is the new Zion. They are also appropriate for church celebrations such as parish anniversaries and for occasions of prayer for social justice in this world.

## Special Groups of Psalms

There are other sets of psalms. Psalms 43 through 83 all refer to God as *Elohim* rather than Yahweh, the personal name of God, indicating that they are from the same collection. Psalms 120 to 134 are *pilgrim* or "gradual" (step) songs. They are all headed "A Song of Ascents," probably because they were sung on the way to Jerusalem, either for the festivals of Passover, Pentecost, and Tabernacles or on the return north from exile in Babylon. Even when Jerusalem was south, people spoke of going "up" to this holy city 2,600 feet above sea level, where they felt God dwelt in a special way. Another hypothesis is that these psalms were prayed ascending the fifteen steps that led from the Court of Women to the Court of the Israelites in the Temple.

♪ psalm notes...

Iceland's national anthem is based on Psalm 90.

# Adapting the Psalms for Christians

*"For God is king of all the earth; sing praises with a psalm."*
Psalm 47:7

aint Jerome's saying "Ignorance of Scripture is ignorance of Christ" applies to the psalms in a very special way. The psalms are centered on the loving, saving action of God in the world, and therefore they are centered on Christ, who is the Word of God and our loving Savior. The "cry and rescue" history of Israel culminates in the Messiah, the "Anointed One," whom God sent to save the human race. For Christians, the psalms reach their fulfillment, their meaning becomes clear, they blossom, in the New Testament, which quotes the Book of Psalms more than any other Old Testament book, citing a total of 116 psalm verses. Jesus walks through the psalms as surely as he walked the paths of Galilee. But sometimes we have to search for him as in *Where's Waldo?* or in the visual puzzles you stare at until the hidden picture emerges. In addition, the psalms and Jesus share a common function: both reveal what it is like to be truly and completely human.

## Messianic Psalms

One reason the psalms appear so frequently in the Gospels is that some of them foretell of the Messiah, the new king or leader who would come to save Israel and who at the end of the world will come again to judge the earth. The Gospel writers (in particular Matthew, who has 21 psalm references) were eager to show that the psalms prove Jesus is the long-awaited

St. Francis of Assisi's favorite Bible verse, "He drew me up from the desolate pit, out of the miry bog, and set my feet upon a rock" (Psalm 40:2), was the model for his life of loving compassion. Francis died singing Psalm 141.

Messiah. They incorporated verses that can be interpreted as referring to Jesus and perhaps sometimes shaped accounts of his life to fit other verses. For example, the similarity between Mark's story of the crucifixion (Mark 15) and Psalm 22 is remarkable.

Jesus himself gives credibility to viewing the psalms as prophetic. On Easter night when he appeared to his apostles, he declared, "Everything written about me in the law of Moses, the prophets, and the psalms must be fulfilled" (Luke 24:44). He singled out the psalms as writings that reveal him. In the same spirit, the Church finds Christ in certain verses. For example, "Even my bosom friend in whom I trusted, who ate of my bread, has lifted the heel against me" (Psalm 41:9) is seen as a reference to Judas. The Church reads Psalm 16:10, "For you do not give me up to Sheol, or let your faithful one see the Pit," as a hint of Christ's resurrection. She uses the verse "God has gone up with a shout, the LORD with the sound of a trumpet" (Psalm 47:5) in the liturgy for the Ascension. In what must have been quite a mental exercise, Saint Augustine, popular bishop of Hippo in North Africa in the early fifth century, managed to give homilies in which he explained each of the 150 psalms in light of the mystery of Christ.

It is important to remember that Catholics are not literalists or fundamentalists when it comes to the Bible. We understand that the Scriptures were written by human beings, under divine inspiration, over hundreds of years, in reaction to specific historical occurrences in Hebrew history. The fact that Christians see Christ reflected in the psalms is not "proof" (as in a court of law) that Jesus was the Messiah that the Jews have awaited for centuries. In fact, most Jews did not believe at the time that Jesus was that Messiah and do not believe so today. So Christians are reading the psalms with the eyes of faith, and when we do so we see that Jesus, who was most certainly a Jew, fulfilled all the best hopes and longings and promises of his people, as reflected in their own Scriptures, including the psalms.

## Christians' Use of Psalms

Jesus, the founder of Christianity, was steeped in the psalms. He grew up praying them at home, in the local synagogues, and in the Temple services. Because in the Hebrew culture women didn't learn to read, no doubt his mother, Mary, knew many psalms by heart. The Gospels, which refer to forty different psalms, depict Jesus as quoting them on several occasions. Most memorably, as Jesus hangs on the cross he prays, "My God, my God, why have you forsaken me?" (Psalm 22:1) and "Into your hands I commend my spirit" (Psalm 31:5). Even the devil quotes a psalm (Psalm 91:11-12) during his temptation of Jesus! Satan wheedles, "...for it is written, 'He will command his angels concerning you,' and 'On their hands they will bear you up, so that you will not dash your foot against a stone'" (Matthew 4:5-6).

The earliest Christians were Jewish, so as part of their spiritual inheritance they took over the entire Old Testament (more sensitively today called the Hebrew Scriptures)—complete with the psalms. Monsignor Ronald Knox facetiously dubbed the psalms "the Church's nursery rhymes." At first, when Christians were still considered a Jewish sect, they participated as usual in the Temple worship, which included psalms. Later in their own services the Christians "baptized" the psalms by concluding each one with the Glory Be to the Father, a doxology of the Trinity. When praying the psalms evolved into saying the Divine Office, Christians appended a prayer to most psalms that cast them in a Chris-

♪ psalm notes...

Psalm 117 is "the gospel psalm" because it is quoted in Romans 15:11 to explain why the gospel should be preached to the Gentiles.

37

The Lectionary, the book of readings used in Christian liturgies, incorporates 84 of the 150 psalms as responsorial psalms. These psalms are a reaction to the first readings in harmony with the readings to follow.

tological light. For example, after Psalm 20, which is "a prayer for victory for the king in time of war," we pray, "LORD, you accepted the perfect sacrifice of your Son upon the cross. Hear us during times of trouble and protect us by the power of his name, that we who share his struggle on earth may merit a share in his victory."

The psalms are most meaningful for Christians because our God is also the God of the Jews. In fact, it was the Jews who were "chosen" to reveal the true nature of the one God to the world. And it was the Hebrew race that produced humanity's crowning glory, Jesus Christ. Moreover, what the writers of the psalms were is what we are as well. The sentiments expressed by the psalmists are common to all people: wonder, adoration, love, joy, gratitude, guilt, relief, fear, terror, pain, contrition, frustration, anger, rage, and yes, even hatred. John Calvin said that the psalms were an "anatomy of all parts of the soul, for no one will find in himself a single feeling of which the image is not reflected in this mirror." In other words, the psalms are universal and always timely.

### How Christians Pray the Psalms

Like Jews (and Muslims), Christians praise God. We can't help ourselves! Praise is our rock-bottom, honest, human response to our encounter with and experience of divine life. We speak for all created things that have no voice to praise our Creator. Like our Jewish ancestors, when in danger we appeal to God for help and when repentant we turn to God for forgiveness. The psalms usually express what is in our hearts better than our own words can. Praying them is comparable to performing a Chopin piece on the piano, instead of a song we ourselves have composed.

God does not need our prayers of praise and thanks, however. The inscrutable, all-wise God is self-sufficient. Why then do we pray in adoration? First of all, because it is human nature to acknowledge goodness when we see it, and God, above all others, is good. Moreover, just as one spouse likes to hear the words "I love you" from the other even though it is evident and obvious, God, in whose image we are made, must delight in hearing us state our feelings toward him. Second, we pray prayers of praise because prayer changes *us*. As we reflect on the awesome attributes of God (power, wisdom, loving kindness, mercy, justice) and ponder God's unexplainable passion for us, the fires of our love for God are stoked. And when that happens, we are inspired to imitate our God, who "lifts up those who are bowed down," "watches over the strangers," and "upholds the orphan and the widow" (see Psalm 146:8–9). We begin to reach out to God's other children—especially the poor—with mercy and justice. We "love one another as God has loved us," as Jesus urged us to do.

But why should we pray psalms that ask God for help? God obviously knows when we need help. Surely God's unconditional love would compel him to care for us without our asking. Nevertheless, according to Jesus we are to petition the Father to supply our needs. We are to "ask, seek, and knock" (see Luke 11:9). The same words that the ancient Hebrews used to express *their* needs also fit our situations today. For example, Psalm 64, which probably originally was David's plea to be delivered from the "secret plots of the wicked," is easily adapted to our world threatened by terrorists.

## A New Song

Psalm 96 begins, "O sing to the LORD a new song." Several other psalms refer to singing a new song. When Christians pray the psalms, we are singing a

♪ psalm
notes...

✳ To hear the psalms sung in Hebrew, go to www.HebrewPsalms.org.

new song. Although many psalms can still be prayed with their original meaning, some psalms assume a whole new meaning in a Christian context. The major way that Christians praying the psalms differs from the Jews is that we say the words knowing that the Messiah has come, still lives, and will come again. We are familiar with the story of Jesus' life and have personally experienced him acting in our lives. When the psalms mention distress and pain, we know that we can unite our sufferings to Christ's to infuse them with purpose. When the psalms ponder why evildoers thrive, we know that there is an afterlife where the good will enjoy rewards and the evil will endure punishment. We pray the psalms as songs of the kingdom that Jesus proclaimed, the kingdom that has both already begun here on earth and is also yet to come.

The coming of Christ also imparts a new dimension to many essential themes in the psalms. The covenant, or agreement between God and the Israelites, which made them a people all his own, culminated in the new covenant instituted by Christ. It foreshadows our own baptismal covenant, which unites us with the death and resurrection and mission of Jesus. The liberation from slavery in Egypt that is celebrated in the psalms is a forerunner of God saving us from the slavery of sin and death. The Law admired and loved by the Israelites and sung about in the psalms was enhanced by Jesus' new law of love, which calls us to love one another as he loved us and to love even our enemies. For Catholics, the king and his bride in the psalms are Christ and his beloved Church. The Jerusalem of the psalms develops into the new Jerusalem of the Book of Revelation, the holy city coming down from heaven. In short, graced with the perspective that comes with living in the light of Christ, we pray the psalms with a new twist.

## Some Dissonance

Naturally the differences between the primitive patriarchal and monarchical Hebrew society and our modern society over twenty centuries later pose some problems in praying the psalms. Some Hebrew practices can repulse us or at least make us uncomfortable. Here are a few difficulties and explanations that might alleviate the problems.

*Complaining to God.* The Hebrews had a very personal relationship with God that led them to speak to God as one might speak to another human person. In fact, they spoke as freely to God as to a family member. Recall how Abraham haggled relentlessly with God to spare the city of Sodom (Genesis 18:16–33). It's been noted that no one in the psalms ever says, "Please." In the psalms we find lines such as "Rouse yourself! Why do you sleep, O Lord?" (Psalm 44:23). In the first two verses of Psalm 13,

Recent studies of the psalms focus not so much on the interpretation of individual psalms in the collection but on the psalms as a whole book. The chief theme running through this book is "Yahweh is king."

the psalmist dares to ask the Lord four times, "How long?" The Hebrews vent and complain to God in ways that shock us. We are not accustomed to such bold honesty. On the other hand, at certain crisis times in our lives, it can be cathartic and therapeutic to pray in those words. When circumstances in our life enable us to identify with a lament psalm, we can refer our sorrows, problems, and pains to God. The psalmist teaches us that anything in life is fair game for prayer. And no matter how much the psalmist rants and raves, he trusts that in the end the good God will do what is best.

*Declaring innocence.* In a number of psalms the pray-er protests that he or she is a good person and has kept God's law: For example, "If you test me, you will find no wickedness in me" (Psalm 17:3). Sometimes this proclamation of one's innocence is offered as a reason why God should answer a request. Other times it is embedded in a psalm that questions why bad things are happening to the pray-er, while evil people prosper. We feel uncomfortable addressing God this way, especially since we (and God) know that we haven't always been faithful! These verses smack of self-righteousness, the quality Jesus criticized in the Pharisees. Perhaps we can pray such lines mindful that only by God's grace have we been good. Or we can pray in the name of those saints in the body of Christ who have lived up to those words.

*The cursing psalms.* The "imprecation" psalms, which seethe with violence and vindication, are 7, 35, 58, 59, 69, 83, 109, 137, and 140. Much of Hebrew history involved fighting tribes and nations who worshiped pagan gods. Life was cruel, harsh, and bloody. In an act of profound faith, the Hebrews called on God to destroy their enemies in terrible ways. The extreme example of this is "Happy shall they be who take your little ones and dash them against the rock!" (Psalm 137:9) Another psalm pleads, "O God, break the teeth in their mouths" (Psalm 58:6), and another, "Let their way be dark and slippery, with the angel of the Lord pursuing them" (Psalm 35:6). Obviously followers of the merciful Christ who taught, "Love your enemies," are puzzled and repelled by such violence in Sacred Scripture.

One explanation of the cursing psalms is that the Hebrews were champions of God and fought for his sake. By conquering their pagan enemies, they were conquering God's enemies. Thus, their fervor. Another thought that excuses the cursing somewhat is that the Hebrews were relying on God and God's justice to wreak the violence. They were not taking vengeance themselves, but leaving it to God. Another reason for the violence of these psalms is that the Hebrews suffered incredibly when their holy city Jerusalem was destroyed. In exile in Babylon they wept and, unable to sing, they hung up their harps as Psalm 137 tells us. These cursing psalms of the Hebrews served as a means of teaching their children to always remember these horrors.

Ron Rolheiser, O.M.I., points out that in prayer we lift our hearts to God, and if we are honest those hearts sometimes contain negative feelings. He says, "Feel-good aphorisms that express how we think we ought to feel are no substitute for the earthy realism of the psalms, which express how we actually do feel. Anyone who would lift mind and heart to God without ever mentioning feelings of bitterness, jealousy, vengeance, hatred, and war should write slogans for greeting cards and not be anyone's spiritual advisor."

It's been recommended that when praying the cursing verses you think of "enemies" not in the physical world but in the spiritual world: your own evil tendencies, evil in general, sin, and Satan. In

♪ psalm notes...

"The Psalms arose from the communities of the Holy Land and the Diaspora, but embrace all creation. Their prayer recalls the saving events of the past, yet extends into the future, even to the end of history; it commemorates the promises God has already kept, and awaits the Messiah who will fulfill them definitively. Prayer by Christ and fulfilled in him, the Psalms remain essential to the prayer of the Church." *Catechism of the Catholic Church*, 2586

In February of 1995,
*The New York Times*
reported, "Seeking
solace from his recent
political troubles,
President Clinton said
today that he had just
read the entire Book
of Psalms, hymns that
praise God and often
ask divine relief from
sufferings inflicted by
enemies."

times of sickness, the enemy can be the illness, such as cancer cells or the HIV virus. Then the venomous words in the psalms can be right and Christian, for Jesus himself warred against sin and hated death. An alternate way to pray the cursing psalms is in the way Saint Jerome prayed them: by asking God to destroy one's enemies by converting them into friends.

# The Psalms as Poetry

*"May the words of my mouth and the meditation of my heart*
*be acceptable to you, O LORD, my rock and my redeemer."*
Psalm 19:14

A ll the psalms in the Book of Psalms are poems, many of them written with sublime artistry. Poetry is a good vessel for prayer. This literary form captures the essence of things in powerful language, touches the heart, and is easily memorized. In order to better appreciate and understand the psalms, it helps to understand the poetic form they take. The poetry of the Hebrews' psalms is from the ancient middle east and similar to the poetry of the Hebrews' Canaanite neighbors. Like most poems, psalms pack much meaning in a few words. Their succinctness, however, surpasses that of most English poetry, because Hebrew has no articles like "a" and "the" and no auxiliary verbs. A line of four words in Hebrew might mushroom into four times that many when translated into English. There are other ways that Hebrew poetry is quite distinct from the English poems, sonnets, odes, and limericks we know. Here are its characteristics.

## Hebrew Rhythm

No doubt at one time in English class you scanned poems to determine their meter. Remember learning that Shakespeare's plays were written in iambic pentameter? While European poets arranged their words in patterns of stressed and unstressed syllables, the Hebrews had a system of rhythm based only on stressed words. Usually a verse of Hebrew poetry has two parts (called *stichs* or *cola*), each containing two to four stressed syllables. Of

The psalmist sometimes speaks of taking shelter in the shadow of God's wings (see Psalms 57:1; 61:4; 63:7). Besides conjuring up the image of a protective mother bird and her chicks, the psalm might also refer to two places where the Hebrews believed God was present: the ark of the covenant, on which two winged cherubim faced each other, and the Temple, where cherubim were carved into the walls. The verse foreshadows Jesus saying that he longed to gather Jerusalem under his wings (see Luke 13:34).

course, since most of us read translations, these rhythms are lost to us.

## Idea Rhyme

Rather than sound rhyme, in which sounds are repeated, Hebrew poetry has "idea rhyme." Just as a piece of music often has a theme that is repeated in different moods and keys, the psalms play with ideas—repeating, amplifying, and reinforcing them in various ways. In 1753, Robert Lowth, a bishop of the Church of England and a professor of poetry at Oxford University, pinpointed three main types of Hebrew idea rhyme.

1. A second line in a psalm may echo an idea with almost identical or different words (synonymous parallelism):
   *The LORD is a stronghold for the oppressed,*
   *a stronghold in times of trouble.* Psalm 9:9

   *O LORD, how many are my foes!*
   *Many are rising against me.* Psalm 3:1

2. A second line may express the opposite of the idea (antithetic parallelism):
   *For the LORD watches over the way of the righteous,*
   *but the way of the wicked will perish.* Psalm 1:6

3. A second line may develop the first idea expressed (synthetic parallelism). The new line can simply add information, or it can relate to the first as cause and effect, question and answer, comparison, or contrast:
   *For the LORD is a great God,*
   *and a great King above all gods.* Psalm 95:3

The addition can occur in steps, with the second

line echoing the first and a third line carrying the idea forward:

*Lift up your heads, O gates!*
*and be lifted up, O ancient doors!*
*that the King of glory may come in.* Psalm 24:9

In addition to Bishop Lowth's categories, a fourth type of parallelism has been identified in which one line contains a simile that creates a picture, an image, of the idea expressed in the other line (emblematic parallelism):

*I lie awake;*
*I am like a lonely bird on the housetop.* Psalm 102:7

Also, ideas in the psalms are sometimes presented in an inverted form called a chiasmus, for example, AB-BA or AB-C-BA. In other words, one or more ideas are presented and then reflected back in reverse order, as in a mirror. Psalm 145:20 illustrates this:

(A) *The Lord watches over* (i.e., God's action)
(B) *all who love him,* (i.e., type of people)
(B) *but all the wicked* (i.e., type of people)
(A) *he will destroy.* (i.e., God's action)

## Repetition: More Is More

Sometimes a psalm contains a line or two or even an entire stanza that is repeated, making the psalm especially suitable for singing. Psalm 136, for example, is a litany composed of twenty-six verses, each ending in "for his steadfast love endures forever" like a regular heartbeat. In Psalm 107, verses 6, 13, 19, and 28 are all basically, "Then they cried to the LORD in their trouble, and he saved them from their distress." (See also Psalms 24, 46, 62, 67, 80, and 118.) In Psalm 42, verses 5 and 11 are identical, and the same words occur at the end of Psalm 43, lead-

♪ psalm notes...

According to the figuring of rabbis, the Psalter has 5896 verses. The central verse reads, "Yet he, being compassionate, forgave their iniquity and did not destroy them; often he restrained his anger and did not stir up all his wrath" (Psalm 78:38). So at the heart of the psalms lies a verse about God's mercy, a theme repeated throughout Scripture.

In the times of the psalms, after a war the victor would place his foot on the prostrate conquered king. That is why some psalms refer to making an enemy a footstool.

ing us to think that the two psalms originally were one, with a refrain.

Psalm 118 exhibits three other types of repetition found in Hebrew poetry. It has *inclusio*, which means that words or ideas at one point are repeated later to form a frame. For instance, "O give thanks to the LORD, for he is good; his steadfast love endures forever," is verse 1 as well as verse 29, the last verse. This psalm also demonstrates *anaphora*, in which words at the beginning of lines are repeated: "It is better to take refuge in the LORD/than to put confidence in mortals. It is better to take refuge in the LORD/ than to put confidence in princes" (verses 8–9). Psalm 118 also contains the opposite of anaphora, *epiphora*, in which words at the ends of lines are repeated. Verses 10, 11, and 12 all have as the second part: "in the name of the LORD I cut them off!"

### Imagery: Word Pictures

Like all poetry, the psalms are shot through with vivid, concrete images that evoke emotions. At times the language is utterly charming. For example, Psalm 56:8 presents God as lovingly gathering and saving our tears in a bottle. Then there is the exquisite verse "You knit me together in my mother's womb" (Psalm 139:13) and the poignant "As a deer longs for flowing streams, so my soul longs for you, O God" (Psalm 42:1). Anyone in serious trouble can immediately identify with the psalmist's description "The waters have come up to my neck. I sink in deep mire, where there is no foothold" (Psalm 69:1–2). In the psalms enemies "lick the dust" (Psalm 72:9), a sinner can be washed and made "whiter than snow" (Psalm 51:7), and daybreak is "the womb of the morning" (Psalm 110:3).

Similes, that is, comparisons that use the words

## *God Presented Poetically*

Allow the psalms to stretch the ways you think about God. The psalms depict God through creation imagery: God is "wrapped in light as with a garment" (Psalm 104:2). The clouds are his chariot, and he rides on the wings of the wind (see Psalm 104:3). God "utters his voice, the earth melts" (Psalm 46:6), and "the mountains melt like wax before the LORD" (Psalm 97:5). "As the mountains surround Jerusalem, so the LORD surrounds his people" (Psalm 125:2).

The psalms describe God as a rock, a stronghold, a fortress, a shield, a warrior with sword and arrows, and a place of refuge. A thousand years to God is "like a watch in the night" (Psalm 90:4). (A watch was three hours.) God punishes by "consuming like a moth what is dear to them" (Psalm 39:11). God's "steadfast love is as high as the heavens" and his "faithfulness extends to the clouds" (Psalm 57:10). The promises of the Lord are "silver refined…purified seven times" (Psalm 12:6), and the precepts of the Lord are "sweeter also than honey" (Psalm 19:10).

♪ psalm notes…

Many people call on Saint Anthony for help in locating something lost, but few know why he is the patron saint of lost articles. It is said that one day a novice stole Anthony's Psalter and left the community. This was especially upsetting to Anthony because of all the notes he had made in the margins. Eventually Anthony's Book of Psalms was returned, and the novice rejoined the community. Thus the lost was found, and Anthony had his special job.

*like* or *as*, abound. Visualize the following images found in laments. The poet is "like a broken vessel" (Psalm 31:12), "like a lonely bird on the housetop" (Psalm 102:7), "poured out like water" (Psalm 22:14), "gone like a shadow at evening" and "shaken off like a locust" (Psalm 109:23). The psalmist's soul is "like a weaned child with its mother" (Psalm 131:2), and he says to God, "My soul thirsts for you like a parched land" (Psalm 143:6).

Curses in the psalms are as colorful as Irish curses: "Let them be like chaff before the wind" (Psalm 35:5), "Let them be like the snail that dissolves into slime" (Psalm 58:8), and "Let burning coals fall on them!" (Psalm 140:10).

Chilean poet Pablo
Neruda (1904–1973)
wrote, "Poetry is a
deep inner calling in
man; from it came
liturgy, the psalms,
and also the content
of religions."

Creation is creatively described: "You stretch out the heavens like a tent" (Psalm 104:2). The sun "comes out like a bridegroom from his wedding canopy, and like a strong man runs its course with joy" (Psalm 19:5). "He hurls down hail like crumbs" (Psalm 147:17). "The mountains skipped like rams, the hills like lambs" (Psalm 114:4), and "Then shall all the trees of the forest sing for joy" (Psalm 96:12). "The meadows clothe themselves with flocks, the valleys deck themselves with grain, they shout and sing together for joy" (Psalm 65:13). Mortals "are like a breath; their days are like a passing shadow" (Psalm 144:4).

Enemies in the psalms are "with speech smoother than butter" (Psalm 55:21), and "they lurk in secret like a lion" (Psalm 10:9). "Pride is their necklace; violence covers them like a garment" (Psalm 73:6). Their "teeth are spears and arrows, their tongues sharp swords" (Psalm 57:4). They come "howling like dogs and prowling about the city" (Psalm 59:6). They are "like bees; they blazed like a fire of thorns" (Psalm 118:12). The king will "dash them in pieces like a potter's vessel" (Psalm 2:9). Their foot is caught in their own net (see Psalm 9:15). Enemies endure "pains as of a woman in labor" (Psalm 48:6). "Like smoke they vanish away" (Ps 37:20). God calls the country of Moab "my washbasin" (Psalm 60:8).

Morality is presented in terms of walking a path, and stumbling is an image for sinning. God prepares a cup of wine for the wicked, which they will drain "down to the dregs" (Psalm 75:8). Fools who trust in riches are "like sheep...; Death shall be their shepherd" (Psalm 49:14). On the other hand, the psalmist, who trusts not in riches but in God, is like a green olive tree in the house of God (see Psalm 52:8). "The righteous flourish like the palm tree, and grow like a cedar in Lebanon" (Psalm 92:12).

## Acrostic Psalms from A to Z

Some psalms are *acrostic*, that is, each verse begins with a consecutive letter of the Hebrew alphabet, which has twenty-two letters. Acrostic psalms are Psalms 9-10 (which originally might have been a single psalm), 25, 34, 37, 111-112, 119, and 145. This mnemonic device, which makes memorization easier, suggests that these psalms were used in instruction. The ideas expressed in acrostic psalms, however, are often not cohesive but loosely strung together because of the artificial form.

The most fantastic acrostic psalm is Psalm 119, which also happens to be the longest psalm. For each of the twenty-two letters of the Hebrew alphabet (except one), this psalm in praise of God's law has eight verses beginning with that letter. If that weren't amazing enough, each of the 176 verses (except one) contains a synonym for law. Monsignor Ronald Knox in his translation of the psalms accomplishes the same intricate pattern in English.

## Other Literary Devices

Another poetic device used in the psalms is *synecdoche*, a figure of speech in which part of something symbolizes the whole. For example, God's name, God's eye, arm, or right hand is used for God's self. "*Our feet* are standing within your gates, O Jerusalem" (Psalm 122:2) means "*We* are standing."

Similarly, *merism* is also found in the psalms. This is using a few things to represent a whole. For example, in Psalm 66 to explain the awesome deeds God has done, the psalmist in verse 6 states: "He turned the sea into dry land; they passed through the river on foot." These references to the beginning of the Exodus (passing through the Reed Sea), and the end of Exodus (crossing the Jordan) stand

51

for the entire forty-year experience. And Psalm 139:2, "You know when I sit down and when I rise up," means that God knows the psalmist's every move. Again, in Psalm 148:13 when the psalmist exclaims that God's "glory is above earth and heaven," he means above everything.

When Jesus said that if our eye causes us to sin we should pluck it out, he was employing another trait of Hebrew speech, *hyperbole* (exaggeration). It too flavors the psalms of his ancestors. For example, each evening enemies come back "howling like dogs" (Psalm 59:6) and "My eyes waste away because of grief" (Psalm 6:7). The righteous will "bathe their feet in the blood of the wicked" (Psalm 58:10). Enemies number in the tens of thousands, in other words, an infinite number.

*Paronomasia*, a fancy name for pun, is word play through the repetition of words similar in sound, but not necessarily in meaning. Examples in English are "the bear couldn't bear the sight," and "the heart of the hart beat rapidly." The Israelites' love of puns is evident in the psalms. Of course, these puns do not always carry over in translations. For example, we would never guess that in "You have kept count of my tossings; put my tears in your bottle (Psalm 56:8), *tossings* and *bottle* in Hebrew are spelled different but pronounced the same.

*Onomatopoeia*, where the pronunciation of a word echoes the sound it stands for, also occurs in the psalms. For instance, Psalm 1:2, contains the words "on his law they meditate." The Hebrew word translated "meditate" is *hagah*, which actually means "muttering" or "growling." When saying "hagah," which is pronounced deep in the throat, we sound as if we're muttering or growling. In Psalm 127 about building a house, the first couplet contains four words beginning with "b," imitating the sound of a builder's mallet.

## Improvising with the Psalms

Just as God gave us creation to play in, God gave us the psalms for our delight. Several people have engaged in mental games with the psalms, translating them into different forms. Fr. Richard Gwyn has rewritten the psalms as haiku in his book *The Psalms in Haiku* (Ulysses Press, 1998). John Piña Craven has captured their emotions in another form of Japanese poetry, the *tanka*. His psalms, grouped according to theme, can be found at www.aloha.com/~craven/psaltere.html. Norman Fischer, a Buddhist priest, has written a book *Opening to You: Zen-Inspired Translations of the Psalms* (Penguin Putnam, Inc., 2002). Fr. Desmond O'Donnell and Sr. Maureen Mohen have taken New Testament verses and put them into psalm form in *Praying the New Testament as Psalms*. How might you play with the psalms?

Saint Ambrose (c. 303–397) wrote, "A psalm is a blessing on the lips of the people, praise of God, the assembly's homage, a general acclamation, a word that speaks for all, the voice of the Church, a confession of faith in song."

# Becoming Well-Versed in the Psalms

*"I will bless the LORD at all times;*
*his praise shall continually be in my mouth."*
Psalm 34:1

ince Scripture is the word of God, reading the psalms puts us immediately in the presence of the divine spirit, opening the lines for communication. Our purpose in praying the psalms is not to get something from God: more money or fame, not even better health or greater success in our work. Our goal is much higher: to seek God himself. This ultimate quest is satisfied through these song-prayers, where God lives, breathes, and speaks. The Trappist Thomas Merton wrote a book on the psalms called *Bread in the Wilderness*. In it he explained that the psalms nourish us just as the Eucharist nourishes us. God is present in both word and Eucharist to strengthen and guide us. Finding him in Scripture, though, requires some effort.

## The Pitfalls of Translations

The original manuscripts of the Bible no longer exist. From the first documents, these writings were copied over and over again by scribes, and thus human error was introduced. (For one reason, changing one small stroke of a Hebrew letter can create a different word.) Later, of course, the books of the Bible were translated into different languages. There is a somewhat extreme saying, "Every translation is a betrayal," which itself proves the point. In its original Italian this saying is *"Traduttore, traditore."* When this two-

♪ psalm
notes...

Saint Ambrose point-
ed out that birds sing
at dawn and dusk
and that therefore es-
pecially appropriate
times to pray the
psalms are morning
and evening. Psalms 3
and 5 are good morn-
ing prayers, while
Psalms 4, 6, 90, and
143 are fitting for the
end of the day. Inci-
dentally, Psalm 111
makes a good meal
prayer.

word saying is translated into English, the play on words (as well as the music of the Italian) disappears.

To say that the Hebrew of the psalms is a challenge to translate is an understatement. This language has no vowels, so translators have to rely on what they knew about ancient writings (and sometimes on their plain common sense) to determine if, for instance, a word is *lid* or *lad*. They also have to determine the meaning of *homographs*, words that have two or more meanings. In English, for example, *temple* can mean a place to worship or the side of the forehead. We usually can understand which is meant from the context. Likewise, *lie* can be a noun or a verb. Hebrew has similar double-duty words. To complicate matters, Hebrew writing uses no punctuation or spaces between words. To illustrate, in English—with no spacing between the letters—NOWHERE could mean "now here" or "no where." Quite a big difference! In fact, the words are opposite in meaning. Another drawback is that some Scripture texts we have inherited are "corrupt" (incomplete or puzzling), but fortunately these are minor glitches.

The writings of other ancient peoples continue to guide scholars. In 1928 a farmer in Syria discovered a tomb from the ancient city of Ugarit. This led to the finding of Ugaritic writings from the 15th century B.C. that shed light on the writings of the Hebrews, who were neighbors although separated by two centuries. The 1947 discovery of the Dead Sea Scrolls of biblical writings from before 100 A.D. was another boon to translators.

### Choosing a Bible Translation

You might want to compare Bibles and choose your favorite. Some Bibles are translations directly from the first language of the Bible, while others are a translation of a translation. Some Bibles are literal translations of the original words and retain the idioms of Hebrew. Other Bibles have "dynamic equivalence," which means they seek to translate the psalms "sense for sense" rather than "word for word."

Some versions are broad paraphrases in the language of contemporary people, an attempt to make Scripture more understandable. For example, Psalm 10:4 reads that the wicked speak "in the pride of this nose." Various translations render this odd expression "in arrogance," "in the pride of their countenance," "in their insolence the wicked boast," or simply, "the wicked man boasts." To further demonstrate how translations vary, here is Psalm 2:1 as found in several Bibles:

♪ psalm notes...

In the Jewish tradition, after a person dies someone keeps watch at the body and recites psalms constantly until the burial. This service may be done by a relative or arranged by a funeral home.

*Why do the nations conspire,*
*and the peoples plot in vain?*
(New Revised Standard Version)

*Why do the nations rage*
*and the peoples utter folly?*
(New American Bible)

*Why this uproar among the nations,*
*this impotent muttering of the peoples?*
(New Jerusalem Bible)

*Why do the heathen rage,*
*and the people imagine a vain thing?*
(King James Bible)

*Why the big noise, nations?*
*Why the mean plots, people?*
(The Message)

Psalm 91 is known as the soldier's prayer because it expresses confidence in God's loving protection. Troops prayed this psalm in World War I. When actor Jimmy Stewart left for the Army Air Corps and twenty combat missions in World War II, his father gave him this psalm with a letter. Jimmy reported that at the height of battles he drew much comfort from his tattered copy of this psalm. Years later, soldiers going to Iraq are taking with them laminated cards and bandanas imprinted with this prayer.

### How Catholic and Protestant Bibles Differ

Although both Catholic and Protestant Bibles include the Psalms, they differ in that Catholic Bibles have additional books: Judith, Tobit, Wisdom, First and Second Maccabees, Baruch, and portions of Esther and Daniel. These books were part of the Septuagint, the Greek translation of the Old Testament made in Alexandria, Egypt, between the third to first century B.C. Catholics consider them *deuterocanonical* (the second canon or list of inspired books), while Protestants consider them *apocryphal* (not canonical or inspired). Today Christians can share a common Bible that includes these additional books and is approved by both Catholic and Protestant authorities. One example is the New Revised Standard Version, which is the translation used for most of the Scripture quoted in this book.

All Bibles contain the Book of Psalms. You can also find copies of the psalms published separately, apart from the Old Testament. (See the Annotated Bibliography for selected versions of Bibles and Psalms.)

### Fifteen Time-Tested Tips for Reading Psalms

1. If you want the psalms to become more meaningful for you, you must first of all become more familiar with the rest of the Bible. The themes, symbols, and events found in the psalms occur in other places in Scripture. For example, knowing the separate stories of David the King and Jesus the Messiah can make you sensitive to the overtones of the royal psalms. So read and study the whole Bible, both Testaments. When possible, read books, attend lec-

tures and courses, and join Bible study groups at your parish or workplace.

2. Carve a set time in your day for reading the psalms, a time when your mind is free to concentrate on them. You might light a candle (symbol of Christ the light of the world) or burn incense to create a prayerful ambiance.

3. Make a plan for reading the psalms and do your best to stick to it. Putting a check on a calendar when you've done the reading is a good way to motivate yourself. You might concentrate on just one psalm a day, or you might read three a day. You might proceed through the psalms in order, or you might delve into them thematically: first the praise psalms, then the laments, and so on. Or you might use a book or a web site that guides your reading of the psalms.

4. Begin with a prayer to the Holy Spirit, who is sometimes called "the love song between the Father and the Son." This can be the brief invocation "Come, Holy Spirit, fill the hearts of your faithful and enkindle in them the fire of your love." Or you can make up your own prayer.

5. Expect God to speak to you. Louis Evely in his book *That Man Is You* describes how to approach Scripture by referring to the story of the woman in a crowd who merely touches Jesus' cloak and is healed. Evely points out that although many people that day touched Jesus, no one was cured but her. He says that we need to read Scripture the way we'd have touched Christ—with the same reverence, the same faith, the same expectancy that the woman had.

6. Some Bibles provide footnotes with all sorts of helpful information. Read those that go with the psalms. They may explain certain words and expressions. For example, in my Bible a

♪ psalm notes…

"The Psalter is the book in which The Word of God becomes man's prayer." *Catechism of the Catholic Church*, 2587

Saint Ambrose
(c. 303–397) in his
*Commentary on
Psalm I* wrote:
"Psalmody is the
rewarding work of the
night, the grateful
relaxation of the busy
day, the good
beginning and the
fortifying conclusion
of all work. It is the
ministry of angels, the
strength of the
heavenly host, the
spiritual sacrifice."

footnote reveals that the sea and rivers referred to in psalms are the Mediterranean Sea and the Euphrates River and its tributaries. Another footnote informs me that the horn mentioned often in the psalms means not a trumpet but the horn of a bull or wild ox, a symbol of power and strength. Some footnotes give alternate and literal translations. For example, in Psalm 59:1, the words "protect me" from my enemies actually in Hebrew are "Lift me high above their heads." Footnotes also alert us to words and verses where the meaning is uncertain.

7. Bibles may indicate cross-references for passages. You might look these up to enrich your reading. Some cross-references lead to places in the Old and New Testaments where the same or similar words occur. Others direct you to an explanation of a verse. For example, the reference for "He turned the sea into dry land; they passed through the river on foot" (Psalm 66:6) is Exodus 14:21 ff, which tells the story of the Israelites passing through the Reed Sea.

8. In the past there was no such thing as silent reading. Instead, people read aloud, which involves more senses because you form the words with your mouth and hear them with your ears. Consequently, reading psalms aloud makes them more striking. You can do this in various ways. Read psalms loudly as a proclamation or whisper them. Stress certain words to highlight different meanings. Notice how the meaning of Psalm 27:1 changes as different words are stressed: "The LORD is my light." "The Lord IS my light." "The Lord is MY light." and "The Lord is my LIGHT." If you don't pray the psalms aloud, at least move your lips.

9. Since the Bible is God's word to us and therefore a book drenched in love, read the psalms as

you would read a love letter—slowly and thoughtfully, lingering over the words, repeating phrases and words over and over, relishing each line, and committing the words to memory. Read between the lines and milk the words for hidden meanings. Wonder what private message God is sending you. Poet Rainer Maria Rilke wrote that a reader "does not always remain bent over his pages; he often leans back and closes his eyes over the line he has been reading again, and its meaning spreads through his blood."

10. Personalize your Psalter by writing in it. As someone said, "A person whose Bible is falling apart usually isn't." Jot down notes in the margins: insights, questions, and prayers. Highlight, underline, circle, and star key words and phrases. For example, in his personal Bible the composer Bach underlined in 1 Chronicles that musicians are to "express the Word of God in a spiritual songs and psalms, sing them in the temple, and at the same time to play with instruments." In the section on the Psalms, Bach underlined commentary that describes two prophets serving King David by playing musical instruments as part of their official duties.

11. Read the words in context to get a fuller, more correct understanding. In part, Psalm 14:1 states, "There is no God," but the words preceding this declaration are "Fools say in their hearts." In this case, the context negates the statement. In other cases, the context clarifies a phrase.

12. Compare translations of the psalms. You might find that one version is better suited to you and your life or simply more to your liking. You might even try rewriting a psalm in your own words, to see what it really says to you.

♪ psalm notes...

"From the time of David to the coming of the Messiah, texts appearing in these sacred books show a deepening in prayer for oneself and in prayer for others. Thus the psalms were gradually collected into the five books of the Psalter (or "Praises"), the masterwork of prayer in the Old Testament."
*Catechism of the Catholic Church*, 2585

When the psalmist asks that God's face shine on his people, he is asking that God smile on them with favor.

13. Read a commentary on the psalms, a book that breaks open Scripture. (See the Bibliography for some commentaries.) The new information you collect from commentaries will deepen your understanding and appreciation of the psalms, although they are no substitute for reading them yourself.

14. Delve deeper into your favorite psalms. Don't just think, "Psalm 23, I know that one" and skip over it. Read it anew carefully and you'll find that different aspects of the psalms will be revealed. The psalms grow along with you as you bring to them new personal experiences and attitudes. It is a great exercise to memorize all or part of a psalm. You can really "wow" people if you recite a psalm by heart at an appropriate time. Or you can just use it as a prayer on your own at any time.

15. Vary how and where you read the psalms. For example, you might take a prayer walk and pray a few psalms along the way. Or, if you usually read the psalms sitting in a chair, kneel or stand for a change. Insert bows at appropriate places. You might invest in a prayer pillow, a prayer rug, a prayer kneeler, or a prayer stool.

## Senses of the Psalms

One way to read the psalms is to think about what they originally meant to the Israelites who wrote and sang them. This is where knowledge of the rest of the Old Testament and the culture of the Israelites comes in handy. To the Hebrews the psalms were a declaration of the saving power of God, a personal God about whom they could boast, "What other great nation has a god so near to it as the LORD our God is whenever we call to him?" (Deuteronomy 4:7). To pray the psalms as the Hebrews prayed them is certainly valid and also very beautiful and satisfying.

Beyond this, the psalms can also be read in light of the New Testament, what is known as the "fuller sense." That is, Christians believe that many verses refer to Jesus. "The stone that the builders rejected has become the chief cornerstone" (Psalm 118:22) describes Jesus. Other verses are related to his life. "They have pierced my hands and my feet" (Psalm 22:16 in some translations) and "For my thirst they gave me vinegar to drink" (Psalm 69:21) refer to his crucifixion. His resurrection from the dead is hinted at in Psalm 16:9–11, and his coronation at God's right hand is found in Psalm 110:1–3. The royal wedding psalm, Psalm 45, is regarded as a reflection on the union of Christ and his Church.

In addition to taking the psalms at face value (that is, literally), we can also read them for deeper implications. Scripture scholars have proposed three levels of spiritual meanings. We can interpret verses as types or figures that foreshadow Christian entities. We can read them for their ethical meaning, their connection with moral conduct. And we can read them for their eschatological meaning, that is, their reference to God's kingdom here and not yet. Take, for example, the word *Jerusalem*. Literally it stands for the historical city in the Holy Land. But it can also signify the Church, our soul as the seat of virtue, and the kingdom of heaven.

The psalms have many layers. Perhaps the most pertinent meaning a psalm verse has for us at a certain time is the one we read into it regarding our own lives and what we are going through.

## Lights, Cameras, Action!

The psalms are packed with word pictures worthy of a Steven Spielberg film. As you pray, use your imagination to make these pictures appear in living

♪ psalm notes...

When a psalm depicts God as riding the clouds, it is applying to Yahweh a title of Baal, a Canaanite god, who was known as the Rider of Clouds. This image is sometimes tied to the Ascension of Jesus.

The readings for daily Mass, including the Responsorial Psalm, are available as both text and audio at www.usccb.org/nab/nabpodcast.shtml.

color and play out on the screen of your mind's eye. The psalms will become vivid and memorable, and your attention will be grabbed.

Picture a beautiful girl being clothed by her maids with in a colorful gown, cloak, and veil all shot through with glittering gold. Then see her gliding down the hall led by the courtiers and followed by a bevy of excited young women. Visualize her approaching the mighty king who is crowned and seated on his throne:

*The princess is decked in her chamber*
*with gold-woven robes;*
*in many colored robes she is led to the king;*
*behind her the virgins, her companions, follow.*
Psalm 45:13–14

In the following verses, God is presented as a mighty warrior against evil. Picture God sharpening a sword on stone. Then see him stand a large bronze bow on the ground and bend it to fit the string. See him string an arrow through a bow, and then set fire to the arrow:
*God will whet his sword;*
*he has bent and strung his bow;*
*he has prepared his deadly weapons,*
*making his arrows fiery shafts.* Psalm 7:12–13

Now hear God speaking in a mighty voice, "Let there be," into a vast void and watch it fill up splendidly with stars, planets, and moons. Then see God scooping immense quantities of water and pouring it into empty land basins and ravines to form oceans, seas, and lakes:
*By the word of the LORD the heavens were made,*
*and all their host by the breath of his mouth.*
*He gathered the waters of the sea as in a bottle;*
*he put the deeps in storehouses.* Psalm 33:6–7

Or picture God demonstrating his power and showing that idols are nothing compared to him. God comes down in dark clouds. Fire burns a path before him, destroying his foes. See the great flashes of lightning and feel the earthquakes that reduce mountains to piles of rubble:

*Fire goes before him,*
*and consumes his adversaries on every side.*
*His lightnings light up the world;*
*the earth sees and trembles.*
*The mountains melt like wax*
*before the LORD.* Psalm 97:3–5

So periodically stop and bring your imagination into play to experience what the psalms express. For example, often the expression "God's face shining upon us" appears in the psalms, for instance Psalm 67:1. Dwell on what it must be like to behold God, to bask in God's loving gaze. When you read, "He drew me up from the desolate pit, out of the miry bog" (Psalm 40:2), recall a time when you felt as if you were trapped in an impossible situation and God lifted you out. When you read, "You hem me in, behind and before, and lay your hand upon me" (Psalm 139:5), ponder the omnipresent God who knows you through and through and is always with you, surrounding you with loving care. When you read, "He has wondrously shown his steadfast love to me" (Psalm 31:21), conjure up memories of times God proved his love for you and savor them. And when the psalmist says, "You will tread on the lion and the adder" (Psalm 91:13), see yourself overcoming other dangerous threats.

## Unchained Melodies

Kathleen Norris in her book *Amazing Grace* recalls how after a cancelled flight she was making her

♪ psalm notes...

Leviathan, who appears in two psalms, is a mythological sea monster. It represents the original chaos that existed before creation. Later it was used for a large sea creature. In Jewish folklore, Leviathan eats a whale each day. In modern Hebrew, *Leviathan* is translated "whale."

Saint Ambrose,
Augustine's teacher,
said, "Though all
Divine Scripture does
breathe the grace of
God, sweet beyond all
others is the Book of
Psalms."

weary way from Terminal 1 to Terminal 2 in O'Hare Airport. As she entered the last corridor of glass and steel, the words "I was glad when they said to me, 'Let us go to the house of the LORD!' Our feet are standing within your gates, O Jerusalem" (Psalm 122:1–2) came to mind. She realized that since the hall was curved, preventing her from seeing what was coming, she had to walk on in trust. She prayed the whole psalm.

The more we delve into the psalms and pray them, the more they will become a part of our lives. As we go about our daily tasks, snippets of the psalms will float into minds, making us more God-conscious. For instance, a tree laden with fruit will make us think of those people in Psalm 1 who follow the way of God's law and bear much fruit. A news report on an act of terrorism will call to mind verses like "How long shall my enemy be exalted over me?" (Psalm 13:2), and a spectacular sunset will evoke "The heavens are telling the glory of God" (Psalm 19:1). Gradually, by reading and praying the psalms, we can become people of praise and thanks 24/7.

# Personalizing the Psalms

*"There is nothing on earth that I desire other than you."*
Psalm 73:25

hen I told my friend Rita I was writing a book on the psalms, she promptly responded, "My favorite psalm is 25." Thinking she really meant the Good Shepherd psalm, I said, "Don't you mean Psalm 23?"

"No," Rita said emphatically, "I mean 25," and quoted, "Make me to know your ways, O LORD; teach me your paths. Lead me in your truth." This psalm spoke to her heart, and she embraced it as her special word from the Lord. No one can tell you what your favorite psalm is, and your choice can change often.

Like the rest of the Bible, the psalms are a personal communication of God to us. We pray them not as a means for us to merit a ticket to heaven but as a way of spending time with the great and wonderful God who made and saved us. We should look at the psalms as an opportunity for a loving encounter with God. The "private" meaning of a psalm passage might not be immediately evident. It might strike us later, for God's word can act like a time bomb. As Saint Benedict advises us, listen "with the ears of your heart." Then we will hear God speaking to us and to the events of our life.

## Making the Psalms Refer to You

Many of the psalms address God directly. In those that don't, you can change the pronouns to speak to God, making the prayers more personal. For example, instead of "The LORD is my shepherd, I shall not want. He makes me lie down in green pastures" (Psalm 23:1–2), pray *"You,* Lord, are

Bishops, institutions, and states adopt a motto, often one from Scripture. You can follow their example and choose a motto from the psalms as a lodestar for your life. For example, "My joy lies in being close to God" (Psalm 73:28 NJB) can become your theme song.

my shepherd . . . *You* make me lie down in green pastures." Or change "For God alone my soul waits in silence; from him comes my salvation" (Psalm 62:1) to "For *you* alone, God, my soul waits in silence; from *you* comes my salvation."

One way to make the psalms more clearly your own is to insert your name in the verses. For example, using my first name, *Kathleen*, the psalms sound like this:

❖ "I, *Kathleen*, will sing of your steadfast love, O Lord, forever." (Psalm 89:1)
❖ "I, *Kathleen*, will call to mind the deeds of the Lord." (Psalm 77:11)
❖ "Answer me, *Kathleen*, when I call, O God of my right!" (Psalm 4:1)
❖ "How long, O Lord? Will you forget *Kathleen* forever?" (Psalm 13:1)
❖ "You show me, *Kathleen*, the path of life." (Psalm 16:11)

Psalm 139 sings about God's all-encompassing knowledge and presence. Notice how deeply moving this psalm is when you rewrite it so that God addresses you personally:

Kathleen, *I have searched you and known you.*
*I know when you sit down and when you rise up;*
*I discern your thoughts from far away.*
*I search out your path and your lying down,*
*and am acquainted with all your ways.*
*Even before a word is on your tongue,* Kathleen,
*I know it completely.*
*I hem you in,* Kathleen, *behind and before*
*and lay my hand upon you.*

*Where can you go from my spirit?*
*Or where can you flee from my presence,* Kathleen?
*If you ascend to heaven, I am there;*
*if you make your bed in Sheol, I am there.*

*If you take the wings of the morning*
*and settle at the farthest limits of the sea,*
*even there my hand shall lead you,* Kathleen,
*and my right hand shall hold you fast.*

*For,* Kathleen, *it was I who formed*
    *your inward parts;*
*knit you together in your mother's womb.*
*My eyes beheld your unformed substance.*
*In my book were written*
*all the days that were formed for you,* Kathleen,
*when none of them as yet existed.*

Psalm 139: 1–5, 7–10, 13, 16

♪ psalm
notes...

✴ Saint Augustine
exclaimed, "How my
love for God is
kindled by the
psalms!"

Most psalms are written in the first person. For those that aren't, you might change the pronouns to your name or a first person pronoun:

❖ "God is *Kathleen's (or my)* refuge and strength." (Psalm 46:1)

❖ "O grant *Kathleen (or me)* help against the foe." (Psalm 60:11)

❖ "May God be gracious to *Kathleen (or me)* and bless me and make his face to shine upon me." (Psalm 67:1)

❖ "As far as the east is from the west, so far he removes *Kathleen's (or my)* transgressions from me." (Psalm 103:12)

❖ "*Kathleen's (or my)* help is in the name of the LORD, who made heaven and earth." (Psalm 124:8)

## Creating Dialogue with God

As you pray a psalm, you can also turn it into a more personal conversation by adding your own thoughts or by linking the ideas to your own life. Stimulate ideas by asking yourself questions: What does this mean to me? What is God saying to me

♪ psalm
notes...

There is a psalm project in which artists are invited to portray a psalm in comic strip format at www.communitycomics.com/cc-selah.html.

here? What appeals to me in this psalm? What do I resist in this psalm? Why?

The psalms are a rich source of ideas for personal prayer. Sometimes the Holy Spirit will use a psalm as a catalyst to take you on another track of prayer that you don't even expect. Psalm 23 might unfold in dialogue as follows:

❖ "The LORD is my shepherd." (How grateful I am that you care for me, Lord.)

❖ "I shall not want." (Thank you for all your gifts. Please give me a heart that likes to share with others.)

❖ "He makes me lie down in green pastures." (I'm so happy that spring is finally coming.)

❖ "He leads me beside still waters." (Help our efforts in working for pure water that is accessible to all.)

❖ "He restores my soul." (I praise and thank you for saving me from sin. Bless me that I may remain in the state of grace.)

## Creating Art from the Psalms

For thirty years James S. Freemantle hand-lettered and illustrated the psalms as a gift for his beloved wife, Clara. Flora, fauna, and scenes from India, where he lived, beautifully fill the pages of his book, *The Psalms of David,* which he finished in 1934, the year he died. The project is reminiscent of the illuminated manuscripts painstakingly lettered by monks in the Middle Ages.

Today the Liturgical Press has undertaken a similar work in its Saint John Bible series. With Donald Jackson as artistic director and illuminator, *Psalms* has been produced with striking illustrations that include digital voiceprints of sacred songs from Benedictine, Native American, Muslim, Taoist, and other traditions. On each page a gold image graphically renders the chanting of the monks.

If you know how to do calligraphy, letter a psalm or psalm verse. Otherwise use a graceful font on your computer. Then decorate the words with art (or ask an artistic friend to do so). You might print the verse or verses, highlighting key words by using different colors and sizes. Illustrate the words by adding a photo or a picture done in watercolor or pastels. If you are skilled with the needle, you might embroider or cross-stitch the words. Frame your work and display it in your home or workplace, or give it as a gift.

♪ psalm notes...

Psalm-based reproducible pictures for children to color can be printed from sites accessed by entering "psalms coloring" in the search engine.

## Variations on the Psalms

Write your own psalm, using one of God's as a model. Psalm 23, the world's favorite psalm, has inspired many imitations—even a facetious version for dieters and one for a student balloonist! Another version, an encouragement to slow down, is "A Japanese Psalm 23":

*The Lord is my pacesetter, I shall not rush.*
*He makes me stop and rest for quiet intervals;*
*He provides me with images of stillness,*
  *which restore my serenity.*
*He leads me in ways of efficiency*
  *through calmness of mind.*
*And His guidance is peace.*
*Even though I have a great many things*
  *to accomplish each day.*
*I will not fret, for His Presence is here.*
*His timelessness, His all-importance will keep me*
  *in balance.*
*He prepares refreshment and renewal in the midst*
  *of my activity*
*By anointing my mind with the oils of tranquility*
*My cup of joyous energy overflows.*
*Surely harmony and effectiveness shall be*

Theologian Karl Barth told his students, "Read with the newspaper in one hand, as it were, and the Bible in the other." He meant we should search out the correlations between contemporary events and the substance of the psalms. Who is king today? What is today's Babylon? Who are the evildoers today from whom we need to be delivered? What wonderful event in the news should we be praising God for today? For what contemporary sins and crimes must we ask forgiveness?

the fruit of my hours,
for I shall walk in the peace of my Lord
and dwell in His house forever.

(Author Unknown)

Here is a fourteen-year-old girl's paraphrase of Psalm 23:

God is my world. With him I don't need anything;
He helps me to be calm, he keeps me out of trouble.
He makes me live.
He keeps me cool for him.
Even though it's dark around me,
    he makes me unafraid.
Bad things don't scare me because he is with me.
His hands keep everything all right,
    he has my life mapped out.
He makes me brave in front of people who hate me.
He blesses me. My joy explodes.

(Author Unknown)

And here is an Eskimo version:

The Lord is my master. I am his dog.
He makes me lie down in soft snow;
He leads me across firm ice;
He calls to me encouragingly.
He drives me on good trails because I belong to Him.
Through storms and troubles, I will not be afraid
because He is with me.
My harness is securely fastened.
and his hand is on the sled.
He guards me while I eat, though enemies lurk near.
He doctors my hurts.
My heart overflows with gratitude.
Only kindness and gentle care will be mine
    from the hands of this master
And I will be on his team forever.

(Author Unknown)

Psalms of lament are enticing to paraphrase for those who have much to complain about. One woman wrote a prayer bemoaning the fact that driving home across a bridge from the Bronx to Long Island was such an ordeal. Why was her foot always on the brake? How did the cars with out-of-state license plates get to the tollbooth first? Why was she always in the wrong lane? Another psalm comes from Sister Mary Andrew Miller, SND, who wrote a lament on aging. This is the last verse:

*My Savior, do not delay!*
*Strengthen my hearing; aid my memory;*
*add power to my vision; vigor to my body—*
*thus will I thank you all the days of my life—*
*whatever is left! Amen.*

The thanksgiving hymn, Psalm 136, known as "the great hallel (praise)," is a litany that when personalized becomes a powerful contemporary prayer. In thanking God for creation and for deliverance from Egypt, it repeats "for his steadfast love endures forever" twenty-six times. Make a list of blessings God has bestowed on you, such as "sent me a good friend" or "helped me pass the test." Then thank God for these gifts and favors, using the format of Psalm 136:

*O give thanks to the Lord, for he is good,*
*for his steadfast love endures forever.*
*who* (name a blessing),
*for his steadfast love endures forever,*
*who* (name a blessing),
*for his steadfast love endures forever....*

Psalm 150, too, can be adapted to your life. In its six verses the word *praise* occurs thirteen times as the psalmist summons all creation to adore God with various instruments. Rewrite the psalm using things in your life and your world to "praise him"

♪ psalm notes...

Henry Wadsworth Longfellow wrote his own psalm, called "A Psalm of Life." This is one of his best known and most inspiring poems.

Psalm 144 is com-
posed almost entirely
of other psalms.
Except for the last
section, it is made of
phrases borrowed
from at least sixteen
psalms.

with, for instance, "Praise him with pots and pans, praise him with computer and fax."

You might even write your own acrostic psalm in which the first line begins with the letter A, the second line begins with B, and so on. It's not necessary to start with A or to have twenty-six lines. A variation of this kind of prayer is one built on the letters in your name. (When I had my students do this, for one of her "e's" Maureen wrote, "Eternal rest grant unto you, O Lord!")

You can also choose a psalm verse and make it the first line of your own psalm. Here are some verses that make good starters:

❖ *O sing to the LORD a new song, for he has done marvelous things.* (Psalm 98:1)

❖ *Hear my prayer, O LORD; let my cry come to you.* (Psalm 102:1)

❖ *When the cares of my heart are many, your consolations cheer my soul.* (Psalm 94:19)

❖ *Who is like the LORD our God, who is seated on high?* (Psalm 113:5)

❖ *What shall I return to the LORD for all his bounty to me?* (Psalm 116:12)

❖ *You visit the earth and water it, you greatly enrich it.* (Psalm 65:9a)

Finally, you might create your own psalm by piecing together favorite lines from several of them, creating a kind of patchwork quilt. Here's one example:

*My heart and my flesh sing for joy to the living God.* (Psalm 84:2)

*You are my LORD; I have no good apart from you.* (Psalm 16:2)

*There is nothing on earth that I desire other than you.* (Psalm 73:25)

*Your face, LORD, do I seek.* (Psalm 27:8)

*My soul thirsts for you.* (Psalm 63:1)
*In your presence there is fullness of joy.* (Psalm 16:11)

*Hide me in the shadow of your wings.* (Psalm 17:8)
*Who is a rock besides our God?* (Psalm 18:31)
*I love you, O LORD, my strength.* (Psalm 18:1)

*The LORD is my light and my salvation; whom shall I*
   *fear?* (Psalm 27:1)
*I trusted in your steadfast love.* (Psalm 13:5)
*How precious is your steadfast love, O God!*
   (Psalm 36:7)
*I will bless the LORD at all times.* (Psalm 34:1)

## Psalm Verse in Centering Prayer

Centering prayer, or prayer of the heart, is a contemplative kind of prayer in which we simply focus on God dwelling within us and rest in his presence. Although this may sound too simple to you, it is not cheating. On the contrary, contemplation is the highest form of prayer, union with God. For centering prayer, a mantra (a word or phrase that is repeated) carries out two tasks. First it helps you center yourself within, much like the potter centers clay on a wheel. Then during prayer whenever your attention wanders, the mantra recaptures it. The Psalter is an excellent quarry to mine mantras from for centering prayer. A few examples you might use:

❖ "Most High" (Psalm 92:1)
❖ "My refuge" (Psalm 91:2)
❖ "Your name is near." (Psalm 75:1)
❖ "Your way, O God, is holy." (Psalm 77:13)
❖ "My soul longs." (Psalm 84:2)
❖ "You are great." (Psalm 86:10)
❖ "Blessed be the LORD." (Psalm 89:52)
❖ "My rock" (Psalm 92:15)
❖ "Be exalted." (Psalm 108:5).

♪ psalm
notes...

Saint Augustine said in his *Sermon on Psalm 20*, "If the psalm prays, do you too pray; if it laments, so do you too; if it renders thanks, so do you also rejoice with it; if it hopes, so you too; if it speaks in the accents of fear, do you also tremble with it; for all that is written therein is meant to be a mirror for us."

## *Finding the Psalm for the Occasion*

In case of emergency, do you know God's 911 number? It's been identified as Psalm 91:1 and the verses that follow, in which we call on God as our refuge and fortress. The kaleidoscope of our lives generates not only danger and fear sometimes but also a whole spectrum of situations and emotions. The following are suggestions of psalms that harmonize with different occasions or needs. You might pray them to give voice to the movements of your heart.

* When I am in trouble: Psalm 34, Psalm 102
* When a friend has disappointed me: Psalm 55
* When I am happy: Psalm 148
* When I need forgiveness: Psalm 32, 51
* When I feel hopeless: Psalm 13, Psalm 91
* When I am despondent: Psalm 41, Psalm 88
* When I am angry: Psalm 13, Psalm 58
* When I am exhausted: Psalm 69:1–3
* When I am worried or anxious: Psalm 37, Psalm 73
* When I am growing old: Psalm 71, Psalm 92
* When I am the victim of injustice: Psalm 36
* When a friend turns against me: Psalm 41:9
* When I need comfort: Psalm 23, 71
* When I need healing: Psalm 6
* When I am fearful: Psalm 23, Psalm 56, Psalm 91
* When I am discouraged: Psalm 10, Psalm 42
* When I feel lonely: Psalm 71, Psalm 62
* When I need God's guidance: Psalm 27:1, 14; Psalm 32:8
* When my faith is beginning to fail: Psalm 119
* When I want God's protection: Psalm 91
* When I am falsely accused: Psalm 7
* When I am tempted: Psalm 55
* When I lack confidence: Psalm 26
* When people have failed me: Psalm 21
* When it feels as if God is far from me: Psalm 139
* When I am going on a journey: Psalm 121

## Seasonal Psalms

Some psalms are particularly fitting to be prayed at certain times of the liturgical year. The following is a list of correlations:

❖ Advent: Psalms 25, 85
❖ Christmas: Psalm 98
❖ Lent: Psalms 51, 130, 91
❖ Holy Week: Psalm 22
❖ Easter: Psalms 118, 66
❖ Ordinary Time: Psalms 19, 27, 34, 63, 95, 100, 103, 122, 145.

## Other Ideas for Using the Psalms

Here are a few other ideas for making the psalms part of your everyday life:

❖ If the psalms are love letters from God, then it makes sense to answer them. Choose some words from a psalm, ponder what they mean to you, and then write a letter. Begin "Dear God" and let your thoughts flow. Sign it "Love" and your name. You might also write another letter beginning "Dear *(your name)*" and signed "Love, God."

❖ Place a favorite verse where you will see it frequently. You might simply write it on a post-it note and attach it to your mirror, refrigerator, or computer. Or print the verse on a card and insert it in your prayer book or use it as a bookmark in a novel you are reading. You might even find and use (or make!) a calendar with psalms as a theme.

❖ Venerable Bede (c. 673–735), a Benedictine monk and a saint, compiled a popular book of carefully chosen passages from each psalm that he believed represented its essence. Go on a scavenger hunt to locate your favorite psalms or psalms verses in the Psalter. Then assemble them

♪ psalm notes...

In 1995, the Museum of Psalms opened in Jerusalem. It features the paintings of Moshe Tzvi HaLevi Berger, made over the course of fifteen years. The Psalms series has a painting for each of the 150 psalms. These pictures can be viewed at the www. museumofpsalms.com website.

♪ psalm notes...

In 1904, Rowland E. Protero wrote in *The Psalms in Human Life*: "The Book of Psalms contains the whole music of the heart of man, swept by the hand of his Maker…a mirror in which each man sees the motions of his own soul. They express in exquisite words the kinship which every thoughtful human heart craves to find with a supreme, unchanging, loving God."

in a prayer book. You might organize the psalms and verses according to when you will pray them, for example, morning, on special celebrations, when you are depressed, and when you are thankful.

❖ Purchase a beautiful blank book to use as a psalm journal. Then as you pray a psalm, record your thoughts in the journal as well as your own prayers that the psalm inspires you to write. Return to the pages from time to time to nourish your prayer life. You might share passages with a friend.

❖ "Johnny Appleseed" Chapman is best known for planting trees in the lands south of the Great Lakes. Few people are aware that he also planted the seed of God's Word. In his journeys when Johnny stayed at people's homes he often told Bible stories. At the end of his stay, he would leave behind a page from the Bible for the family. You, too, can sow God's Word. In your letters sometimes work in a psalm verse or two. You could also make it a habit to send greeting cards and stationery that have psalms verses imprinted. In your e-mail signature why not include a psalm verse? You never know how God will use this Scripture to touch another's heart.

❖ Have you ever sought God's help by opening the Bible at random and reading whatever words your eyes fall on? If so, you're in good company. When Saint Francis of Assisi was beginning his order, the Franciscans, he opened the Bible three times and found three basic principles for his community's rule of life. Francis called this practice "the first opening." Some call it "Bible roulette." It is said that when Thomas Merton was discerning whether or not to join the Trappist monks, who kept strict silence, he too decided to consult the Bible in this fashion. When he opened it at random, his eyes fell on Psalm 46:10, which in his translation was: "Be silent." This way of using the Bible sounds superstitious to some. But if you really believe that God is present in its words and you approach the Bible with prayer and trust, then this method is an act of faith. The key is to *expect* God to speak to you. It may be, however, that God does not wish to provide you with facile advice or comfort through a "lucky dip" into the Scriptures. Instead you may have to call on your reason, as well other people and the Holy Spirit, to answer your concerns.

♪ psalm notes...

The names of groups who quilt while praying psalms as well as sample patterns for quilting psalms can be accessed by putting "quilting psalms" in a search engine.

# Praying in Concert

*"In the great congregation I will bless the LORD."*
Psalm 26:12

Author Kathleen Norris, a Presbyterian preacher whose extended visits to a Benedictine monastery helped her rediscover her faith, maintains that to sing or say the psalms aloud with a community is to recover religion as an oral tradition. She compares the holiness of the psalms to holding a stone that has been held in the palm by countless ancestors. When we go beyond our individual experience to embrace the pray-ers of the past and pray-ers next to us, we're able to better shape a true vision for the world.

Psalms are communal prayers. They are best prayed in a group (or at least while thinking of oneself as praying them as a member of the believing community). In praying a psalm aloud in community, readers pray slowly, reverently, and clearly. It's important for every person to keep the same pace as the rest for two reasons. First, this avoids distracting and upsetting the other pray-ers. Second, it enables the community to pray with one voice, more perfectly mirroring the unity of the Church on earth and in heaven.

Variety is the spice of spiritual life. Varying the method of praying psalms together not only makes the prayers more interesting but keeps the group alert and focused. Here are a few ideas to try, especially for those who pray the Divine Office daily. As someone observed in regard to praying the psalms, "Familiarity breeds boredom." Taking time to do things a little differently can make a huge difference in the quality of communal prayer. It might also stir up a sense of curiosity and anticipation on the part of those who come together.

On July 20, 2006, fragments of a Psalter from perhaps the eighth century were uncovered by a bull- dozer in a bog in Ire- land, along with part of the leather pouch in which it was kept. So far only part of Psalm 83 is legible.

## Variations in Voices

Psalms are usually sung with the pray-ers divided into two sides, which alternate praying the psalm verses as well as the concluding doxology (Glory Be). These sides can be formed according to how the pray-ers are seated, or in other ways, such as men and women, those over or under a certain age, or even by the first letter of your last name!

Here are some ways to pray the psalms in concert with others:

❖ The community prays an entire psalm in unison.
❖ One person alone prays the whole psalm aloud.
❖ An individual or small group alternates praying verses with a large group.
❖ One person prays or sings each verse, and the community repeats it.
❖ One side prays a verse, and the other side repeats that verse.
❖ One side prays a verse, and the other side prays a refrain.
❖ One person prays the psalm, and the communi- ty prays one line or stanza before the psalm and after each stanza. This refrain can be sung.
❖ For psalms that include dialogue between God and the people or between the leader and the people, one person assumes the role of God or leader.

Here are some variations using music:

❖ The community or an individual sings to a psalm set to music.
❖ All listen to a psalm set to music.
❖ Background music (recorded or live) is played as the psalms are prayed.
❖ Pray-ers sing psalms using Gregorian chant tones.
❖ Pray-ers chant an entire psalm on just one note.

- Pray-ers chant a psalm on one note but drop their voice a third on the last word of each verse.
- All pray silently while a familiar music-only version of the psalm is played.
- All pray or sing a psalm except for one verse that the organ or other instrument(s) "sing."
- Someone or a group does interpretive gestures or dance as the psalm is prayed.

And here are some variations in position:
- Pray-ers pray from different areas of the room. For example, a soloist reads at a lectern, or the chorus stands to one side of the community.
- Pray-ers pray with hands extended and uplifted. This is the *orans*, the prayer posture of the early Christians, Jews, and Gentiles, which is found in ancient drawings. The priest prays this way during the Eucharist, and all now stand this way during the Our Father of the Mass.
- Pray-ers pray standing and facing east. It was the custom for the early Christians to pray facing east, looking to the return of Christ, the Sun of Justice, in glory. At the end of time Christ is expected to come from this direction, as the Advent song "People Look East" attests to. Another reason for facing east is that the sun, a symbol of the Resurrection and a reminder of the Creator, rises from the east.

### Orchestrating a Choral Poem

It seems likely that originally Psalm 135 was prayed as follows: verses 1–4 by chanters, verses 5–14 by one chanter or priest, verses 15–18 by chanters, and verses 19–21 by all. Dividing a psalm like this keeps it from becoming monotonous. A psalm prayed as a choral poem requires planning and training, but after a while a collection builds that can be drawn

♪ psalm notes…

"Lining out" a psalm means that a soloist sings a line and the community repeats it. This was a common way to pray, especially when people were illiterate. The practice was brought to America by the British and the Scots. Many spirituals derived from lining out psalms, beginning in the mid-seventeenth century. Gospel songs were a nineteenth-century descendant of these spirituals but differed from them in that they were harmonized.

upon, especially for special occasions. Set the psalm to be recited as a choral piece with pray-ers taking solo, duet, trio, or group roles. Mark phrases with directions such as "loud," "soft," "sadly," "with gusto." Here is an example using Psalm 118:19–29.

**All** *(loudly):* Open to me the gates of righteousness, / that I may enter through them and give thanks to the LORD.

**Leader**: This is the gate of the LORD; / the righteous shall enter through it.

**Side 1**: I thank you that you have answered me and have become my salvation.

**Solo**: The stone that the builders rejected has become the chief cornerstone.

**All** *(with gusto):* This is the LORD's doing; it is mar-

84

velous in our eyes.

**Solo**: This is the day that the LORD has made;

**All**: let us rejoice and be glad in it.

**Solo** *(plaintively):* Save us, we beseech you, O LORD!

**All**: O LORD, we beseech you, give us success!

**Side 2**: Blessed is the one who comes in the name of the LORD.

**All**: We bless you from the house of the LORD.

**Side 1**: The LORD is God,

**Side 2**: and he has given us light.

**Leader** *(strongly):* Bind the festal procession with branches, up to the horns of the altar.

**Side 1**: You are my God, and I will give thanks to you;

**All**: You are my God, I will extol you.

**Solo**: O give thanks to the LORD, for he is good,

**All**: for his steadfast love endures forever.

♪ psalm notes...

In a speech to the people of the United States after the terrorist attacks of 9/11/01, President George W. Bush incorporated these verses from Psalm 23: "Even though I walk through the valley of the shadow of death, I fear no evil, for you are with me."

Below is Psalm 24 arranged in parts. This psalm is thought to have been sung each year when the ark of the covenant was carried into the sanctuary. Its words are applicable for a procession into any church where the Lord is present today. In praying it, we might also think of heaven, God's dwelling, and the procession of saints entering its gate.

**Solo 1**: The earth is the LORD's and all that is in it, / the world, and those who live in it; / for he has founded it on the seas, / and established it on the rivers.

**Solo 2**: Who shall ascend the hill of the LORD? / And who shall stand in his holy place?

**Solo 3**: Those who have clean hands and pure hearts, / who do not lift up their souls to what is false, / and do not swear deceitfully. / They will receive blessing from the LORD, / and vindication from the God of their salvation. / Such is the company of those who seek him, / who seek the face of the God of Jacob.

Saint Benedict
advised in his Rule
for monks, "Let us so
stand to sing, that our
mind may be in
harmony with our
voice."

*(Cymbal crash or drum roll)*

**Side 1**: Lift up your heads, O gates! / and be lifted up, O ancient doors! / that the King of glory may come in.

**Side 2**: Who is the King of glory?

**Side 1**: *(shouting)* The LORD, strong and mighty, / the LORD, mighty in battle. Lift up your heads, O gates! / and be lifted up, O ancient doors! / that the king of glory may come in.

**Side 2**: Who is the King of glory?

**All**: *(loud and joyful)* The LORD of hosts, / he is the King of glory.

*(Cymbal crash or drum roll)*

## A Unique Way

A group or an individual may find the following way to pray a psalm inspiring and fruitful. First, pray the psalm aloud together. Then have a few moments of silence. Finally, add to the psalm in one of three ways:

❖ repeating a line that is particularly meaningful,

❖ paraphrasing a verse, or

❖ repeating a verse and then adding to it.

Using this method, the praying of Psalm 23:1–4 might sound as follows:

*The LORD is my shepherd; I shall not want.*
*In verdant pastures he gives me repose;*
*Beside restful waters he leads me;*
*he refreshes my soul.*
*He guides me in right paths*
*for his name's sake.*
*Even though I walk in the dark valley*
*I fear no evil; for you are at my side*
*With your rod and your staff*
*That give me courage.*

[Pause]

*Person 1: He refreshes my soul.* (Repetition)
*Person 2: You are at my side.* (Repetition)
*Person 3: He guides me in making right decisions.* (Paraphrase)
*Person 4: Even though I walk through the halls of a hospital, I fear no evil.* (Paraphrase)
*Person 5: I shall not want anything. I'll have all the peace and love I need.* (Addition)
*Person 6: I fear no evil, not even when people try to ruin my reputation.* (Addition)

## A Prayer Service Using the Psalms

For different occasions you may want to prepare a prayer service built on the psalms. The following sample that contains psalms of praise and thanks could be prayed to celebrate the answer to a prayer or an important anniversary:

***Opening Song*** "Lift Up Your Hearts" (Psalm 66) Robert F. O'Connor, S.J.

***Opening Prayer***
*Leader*: Good and loving Father, we come together today to praise and thank you. As our voices declare your holiness and your favors to us, especially *(name a special favor)*, we ask for your grace that we praise you not only in prayer but by our whole life, by our every word and deed. We ask this through Christ our Lord.
*All*: Amen.

***Psalm 67***
Prayed by a soloist.

***Reading*** Revelation 7:9–12

♪ psalm notes...

Most people can probably identify with the story that is told in Psalm 73. The psalmist is struggling with the fact that the wicked seem to prosper while he himself, who is innocent, suffers. Then he goes into the sanctuary of God and realizes that justice will prevail in the end. God holds his right hand, and it is good to be near God.

Igor Stravinsky wrote his Symphony of Psalms to commemorate the fiftieth anniversary of the Boston Symphony Orchestra in 1930. He stated, "It is not a symphony in which I have included Psalms to be sung. On the contrary, it is the singing of the Psalms that I am symphonizing."

### Psalm 145

Sides alternate in praying verses. After each section, all say or sing three alleluias.

### Psalm 96

Sides alternate in praying verses.

### General Intercessions

*Leader*: Let us offer our petitions to our good and gracious God, confident that they will be heard. The response will be: "Father of all, hear our prayer."

God, in your overflowing love, you created us in your image to share your life. Strengthen us to preserve the divine life we receive in the sacraments, we pray to the Lord.

Almighty and wise Creator, you filled the heavens and earth with awesome works. Let us care for them with respect as you envisioned us to, we pray to the Lord.

Compassionate God, you sent your Son to live and die and rise that we might be saved. Give us grace to appreciate this gift and not let it be in vain, we pray to the Lord.

Provident Father, you provide us with food and all necessities of life. Move our hearts to share with one another, especially the most needy, we pray to the Lord.

God of faithful love, you send leaders to guide us in your way. Bless our pope, bishops, and priests that they may have the wisdom and courage to speak and act for you, we pray to the Lord.

Eternal God, you plan to bring us all to live with you in your kingdom. Grant peace and mercy to our deceased family members, relatives, and friends, we pray to the Lord.

*Leader*: Holy and merciful God, we ask these things

in the name of your Son, our Lord Jesus Christ,
and all for your greater honor and glory.
*All*: Amen.

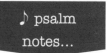
♪ psalm
notes...

### *Prayer*
"The Canticle of Brother Sun and Sister Moon"
by Saint Francis of Assisi (modeled on Psalm 148)

*Most High, all-powerful, all-good Lord,*
*All praise is yours, all glory, all honor*
*and all blessings.*
*To you alone, Most High, do they belong,*
*and no mortal lips are worthy*
*to pronounce your name.*

*Praised be you, my Lord, with all your creatures,*
*Especially Sir Brother Sun,*
*Who is the day through whom you give us light.*
*And he is beautiful and radiant with great splendor.*
*Of you, Most High, he bears the likeness.*

*Praised be you, my Lord,*
*through Sister Moon and the stars,*
*In the heavens you have made them bright,*
*precious and fair.*

*Praised be you, my Lord,*
*through Brothers Wind and Air,*
*And fair and stormy, all weather's moods,*
*By which you cherish all that you have made.*
*Praised be you, my Lord, through Sister Water,*
*So useful, humble, precious, and pure.*

*Praised be you, my Lord, through Brother Fire,*
*Through whom you light the night,*
*And he is beautiful and playful and robust and strong.*

*Praised be you, my Lord,*

Psalm 44 was
carefully written so
that visually it
resembles a zuggurat,
a Babylonian stepped
pyramid.

The book *A Shepherd Looks at Psalm 23* by W. Phillip Keller, which was written over thirty-five years ago, has sold more than two million copies. This beloved book that gives insight into the meaning of the Good Shepherd is still available.

*through our Sister, Mother Earth*
*Who sustains and governs us,*
*Producing varied fruits with colored flowers and herbs.*
*Praised be you, my Lord,*
    *through those who grant pardon*
*For love of you and bear sickness and trial.*
*Blessed are those who endure in peace,*
*By you, Most High, they will be crowned.*

*Praised be you, my Lord, through Sister Death,*
*From whom no one living can escape.*
*Woe to those who die in mortal sin!*
*Blessed are they She finds doing your Will.*
*No second death can do them harm.*
*Praise and bless my Lord and give him thanks,*
*And serve him with great humility.*

***Closing Song*** "Sing to the Mountains"
    (Psalm 118) Bob Dufford, S.J.

### Studying the Psalms

You might want to join or form a Bible study group at your home or parish to begin exploring the psalms. (One recommended program is *The Little Rock Scripture Study* published by Liturgical Press, which offers two good psalm courses with a study guide, a commentary, and a video.) If you prefer not to invest in such a program or if you prefer to study the Psalms alone, you can easily conduct the sessions yourself. Here is a sample format:

1. Read a psalm aloud slowly.
2. Research facts about the psalm: the author, the meaning of the superscriptions, the speaker(s), the category the psalm falls under, when it might be prayed, its poetic characteristics. Many of these can be found in what are called study Bibles or commentaries.
3. Reflect on the gist of the psalm. In a nutshell, what is being said? How does the psalm depict God and the writer of the psalm?
4. Identify verses that are meaningful to you: the ones you like, the ones that apply to your daily life.
5. Refer to a commentary to explain difficult verses.
6. Close by praying the psalm again. You might listen to or sing along with a musical version of the psalm or just pray it as you play instrumental music in the background.

# Singing the Psalms

*"I will sing and make melody to the LORD."*
Psalm 27:6

Saint Augustine said, "To sing belongs to lovers." What better way to pray the psalms, the love songs of God, than to sing them? For, as the English poet William Cowper observed, "Sometimes a light surprises the Christian when he sings."

Scripture orders us to sing to God. The psalmist calls us to "Make a joyful noise to God, all the earth; sing the glory of his name" (Psalm 66:1-2). So does Saint Paul: "With gratitude in your hearts sing psalms, hymns, and spiritual songs to God" (Colossians 3:16) and "Be filled with the Spirit, as you sing psalms and hymns and spiritual songs among yourselves, singing and making melody to the Lord in your hearts, giving thanks to God the Father at all times and for everything in the name of our Lord Jesus Christ" (Ephesians 5:18–20).

C.S. Lewis said, "The most valuable thing the Psalms do for me is to express the same delight in God which made David dance." People ordinarily sing when they are happy. To sing psalms rather than just reciting them gives even fuller expression to our joy in God.

God designed us humans with bodies equipped with five sensational senses. We can praise God with these bodies as well as our spirits. In particular we can pray through song, using the breath and the voice God gave us. Music and dancing can also stimulate our prayer. In the oft-quoted words of Saint Augustine, "Singing is praying twice." (My friend likes to point out that the literal translation of these words is "Singing *well* is praying twice.") Singing requires more energy and involves more senses than speaking words. Consequently it deepens the staying power of words. Also, music

Famous hymn ver-
sions of psalms are
"O God, Our Help in
Ages Past" (Psalm 90)
and "A Mighty
Fortress Is Our God"
(Psalm 46). Hymns
based on Psalm 103
are "Joyful, Joyful, We
Adore Thee," "Praise
to the Lord, the
Almighty," "There's a
Wideness in God's
Mercy," and "Praise,
My Soul, the King of
Heaven."

has the added advantage of drawing a group together. When we sing psalms in community, we enjoy a
foretaste of heaven. For we are joining in the liturgy of heaven where saints and angels continually
sing the Lord's praises.

## A Brief History

Our lack of the original Hebrew melodies of the
psalms has given birth to dozens of beautiful musical settings for them, pleasing people of all ages and
tastes. These versions range from the clear, simple
melodies of Gregorian chant to the pulsing rock
rhythms of a "Psalms Alive" song from Maranatha
Music. Calvin College even offers a CD of jazz vespers (evening prayer with psalms). If you have the
talent and disposition, you might compose your
own original music for a favorite psalm!

In the first century, Saint James taught that
cheerful Christians should sing psalms: "Are any
among you suffering? They should pray. Are any
cheerful? They should sing songs of praise" (James
5:13). We hear from Saint Jerome (345–419 A.D.)
that in his day the farmers of Palestine still sang the
psalms in the fields. The fifth-century bishop, Sido-
nius Apollinaris of Gaul, wrote that boatmen labor-
ing with bent backs to move their barges against
the stream sang psalms until the riverbanks echoed
their hallelujahs.

Originally the psalms were chanted without ac-
companiment in what is called *plainsong* or *plain-
chant*. Gregorian chant got its name because of the
influence of Pope Gregory the Great (540-604) and
became popularized throughout Europe by the efforts of Charlemagne. At first psalms were sung in
*unison* following eight psalm tones, or melodies.
Then in the Middle Ages voices *harmonized* and also
sang in *counterpoint* (different melodies sung to-

gether) and in *organum* (a sustained tone over which the melody was sung by others). Instruments were added, although some faith traditions forbade them.

Beginning in the tenth century, the psalms were the source of the introit, offertory, and communion verses in the liturgy. A psalm called "the gradual" was sung between the readings. It took its name from the step (*gradus*) the leader stood on to sing. The psalms as they were in the Bible were preserved in chant, but this way of singing without a rhythmic pattern or equal number of syllables was difficult.

The Genevan Psalter, published in French in 1542 for the Reformed Church in Switzerland, was the first version of psalms translated with rhymes and set to singable music that was laity-friendly. Later, Isaac Watts, who composed no less than 750 hymns, wrote a collection of metrical psalms. His book *The Psalms of David, Imitated* appeared in 1729 and had the distinction of being the first book Benjamin Franklin published at his own expense.

In 1953, a collection of psalm settings by the French liturgist Joseph Gelineau, S.J., appeared using the French psalms of the Jerusalem Bible. Later he set the Grail Psalms in English to the same melodies. The Grail Psalms had been written by the Grail Society, a lay community, for its own use in 1963. This second version of Gelineau psalms quickly became popular and are still sung.

## Surround Sound

The psalms are favorite material for Christian composers. Many of the hymns in our modern hymnals are psalms put to music or are based on the psalms. For example, "Sing to the Mountains" by Bob Dufford, S.J., is taken from Psalm 118; and "Glory and

♪ psalm notes…

The book *How I Praise You! 150 Little Psalms in Song* by Donna Moss has a verse from each of the psalms set to music for children. For more information go to www.home.earthlink. net/~apex_ps/.

Isaac Watts,
a theologian and
prolific hymn writer in
England, wrote a
poem based on Psalm
98. Lowell Mason, a
Boston choir director,
took this poem and
set it to a melody line
from Handel's
"Messiah." The result
was the popular
Christmas carol "Joy
to the World."

Praise to Our God" by Dan Schutte is drawn from Psalms 66 and 67. "On Eagle's Wings" by Michael Joncas is Psalm 91, and "Rain Down" by Jaime Cortez is based on Psalm 33. In my parish hymnal the psalms listed in the "Index of Scripture Passages Related to Hymns" cover more than four pages—in tiny print. Usually below a hymn there are lines stating which psalms were used. In addition, because responsorial psalms are sung in the liturgy, most publishers of Christian music offer arrangements of these along with dozens of other psalm collections on CDs.

No matter if you don't own a voice like Luciano Pavarotti or Sarah Brightman, it is good to sing Scripture songs. Do you sing in the shower or croon in your car? Do you sing your child to sleep? Why not sing hymns based on the psalms? While praying alone in your room, cleaning, or doing work that doesn't require thought, you might sing a hymn. To bolster your confidence and make you sound better, sing along with a cassette tape or CD. Keep in mind the quotation, "If only the most talented birds would sing, the woods would be silent" and the words of Thomas à Kempis, "If you cannot sing like the nightingale and the lark, then sing like the crows and frogs, who sing as God meant them to."

Even when you are not praying psalms, their music can enhance your prayer. Explore your nearest music store or library for a CD or tape of psalm-based songs to use as an introduction or background for your prayer time. You might also play these songs as you drive, ride a bike, take a bath, walk, or jog.

Plato believed that music both reflects and affects a people's spiritual life. How would you grade the music in your parish? What can you do to enliven it? Here are some tips for singing the psalms in church or any other place:

- ❖ Don't get so carried away by the music that the words become meaningless or secondary.
- ❖ Make a genuine effort to learn new hymns and arrangements based on the psalms.
- ❖ Sing for God's glory, not your own.

♪ psalm notes...

Asteroid 100019 Gregorianik is named for Gregorian chant, using the German short form of the term. The psalms are often sung with Gregorian chant in monasteries and elsewhere.

# Graced Notes
# Psalm Refrains

*"I treasure your word in my heart."*
Psalm 19:11

After the prophet Ezekiel ate a scroll containing the words of the Lord, he declared, "In my mouth it was as sweet as honey" (Ezekiel 3:3). We can savor the words of Scripture just as we savor a piece of hard candy. One way to do this is by praying a mantra, a short prayer—a word, a phrase, or a sentence—repeated over and over. This is sometimes called "prayer of the heart." The psalms are chock-full of possibilities for this form of prayer. I discovered mantras on my own one Christmas night when my father suffered a heart attack and was taken to the hospital where he was anointed. After visiting him and seeing him unconscious and surrounded by machines, I was petrified and couldn't sleep. Then the words "The LORD is my shepherd" (Psalm 23:1) began to echo in my heart, bringing God near and comforting me. Years later when I was undergoing surgery, this same psalm was my strength: "Even though I walk through the valley of the shadow of death, I fear no evil" (Psalm 23:4).

## Why Pray Mantras?

When our eyes are too tired, or too weak, or too tear-filled to pray from the Bible or a prayer book, we can still pray a mantra. When pain, physical or mental, grips us and renders us incapable of expressing a coherent thought, we can still pray a mantra. When we are besieged by irritating problems, burdened with cares, or exhausted by the demands of work, family, and

The first book printed
in British North
America was the
*Bay Psalm Book*. It
was printed in 1640,
in Cambridge,
Massachusetts, just
20 years after the
landing at Plymouth.
The Library of Con-
gress has one of the
ten original copies
still in existence.

friends, we can still find relief and rest in a mantra.

A mantra has gentle power to open us to God and God's action. Its monotonous repetition is as calming and soothing as the rhythm of a rocking chair, a porch swing, or the ebb and flow of waves on the shore. It draws us away from the distractions of daily life and lulls us into a state where we are prepared for an encounter with God.

Just as our measured breathing and rhythmic heartbeats are signs and sources of our natural life, a mantra is an activity of our supernatural life. It brings us into God's presence. Praying a mantra is as simple as a child incessantly crying, "Mommy, I'm sick." Yet it is as meaningful and as beautiful as a lover tirelessly repeating, "I love you." This form of prayer can lead to contemplation and can also transform people. The mantra gradually becomes a part of the person who lets it echo in his or her heart.

## A Long Tradition

Short, repeated prayers have a long history in our faith tradition. In the first centuries of Christianity, hermits kept their minds focused on God and their hearts anchored in God by such prayers. Monks in Egypt prayed over and over, "O God, come to my help" (Psalm 70:1). In the-not-so-distant past, a re-ligious practice was to pray one-line prayers while counting them. I remember as a novice mangling handkerchiefs and praying with the other sisters, "Most Sacred Heart of Jesus, have mercy on us. One. Most Sacred Heart of Jesus, have mercy on us. Two...."

Saint Philip Neri observed, "It is an old custom for the servants of God to have some little prayer ready and to be frequently darting them up to heav-en during the day.... He who adopts this plan will

### Mantras from the Psalter

The Book of Psalms is a goldmine of one-line prayers. Here are a few:

❖ *You are my LORD; I have no good apart from you.* (Psalm 16:2)
❖ *I love you, O LORD, my strength.* (Psalm 18:1)
❖ *Do not be far from me, for trouble is near.* (Psalm 22:11)
❖ *Let your steadfast love, O LORD, be upon us.* (Psalm 33:22)
❖ *God, you are my God, I seek you.* (Psalm 63:1)
❖ *You have been my help, and in the shadow of your wings I sing for joy.* (Psalm 63:7)
❖ *You, O LORD, are a God merciful and gracious.* (Psalm 86:125)
❖ *How great are your works, O LORD!* (Psalm 92:5)
❖ *I give you thanks, O LORD, with my whole heart.* (Psalm 138:1)
❖ *I will praise you, O LORD, as long as I live.* (Psalm 146:2)

♪ **psalm notes...**

Musical settings for psalms occur in the realm of classical music. Leonard Bernstein wrote the choral work *Chichester Psalms*, and Igor Stavinski wrote *Symphony of Psalms*.

get great fruits with little pains."

In recent years the chants of the monks of Taizé have helped make mantras popular once again. The current interest in *centering prayer*, in which mantras play a key role, has also renewed attention to them.

Praying is not only speaking but also listening to God. Some psalm verses are "reverse mantras"—words of God to us. Even verses that do not directly address anyone can become a mantra. For example, the verse "Great is our LORD, and abundant in power; his understanding is beyond measure" (Psalm 147:5) is not *addressed* to God but is *about* God, yet it may be recited as a prayer because it "lifts our minds and hearts to God."

Saint Gregory the
Great said, "God's
word is a melody in
the night."

## How to Pray Mantras

Mantras can be prayed while waiting in a doctor's office or in a checkout line, when put on hold on the phone, while driving or falling asleep. For those of us who crochet or knit, we can pray a different psalm mantra for each row. And, of course, we can also pray mantras during our regular prayer time. Mantras serve to keep us fixed on God. When our mind wanders, the sparse words of a mantra pull it back like a tug on a kite string.

Any posture can be assumed for the praying of mantras. Pray them pacing a room or walking in the woods. Sit in a relaxed position, eyes closed, hands resting on your lap. Let all tension and concerns flow out of you. Recall that God dwells in you. Then slowly repeat the mantra aloud or silently in your heart, synchronizing it with your breathing. If you wish, you can keep track of the mantras with rosary beads.

You may find that as you repeat a short prayer, a word will change and cast a new meaning on what you are saying. For instance, as you pray, "God alone is my rock and my salvation," you may realize suddenly that you are saying, "God alone is my *hope* and my salvation."

One way to pray a mantra is to gradually taper it down. Psalm 46:10 prayed like this becomes "Be still and know that I am God. Be still and know that I am. Be still and know. Be still. Be." Another option is to sing a psalm verse to a well-known tune or your own original melody. Some days you might find that a mantra is the only prayer you can say.

## Psalms by Heart

At the time of Jesus the Old Testament scrolls were kept in synagogues, not homes. This means that when Jesus prayed the psalms, he relied on his memory. It is not unusual for people to have all the psalms stored in their minds. At one time candidates for ordination had to learn the psalms by heart. Also, in the early years of the Church, monks were required to know the Psalter and the whole New Testament by heart. This helped when they gathered to pray at midnight with only candles lighting the chapel.

Janaan Manternach refers to memorizing Scripture verses as "banking prayers." Once psalms or psalm verses are learned by heart, they can be drawn out when needed, or they may rise to the surface automatically. This was Kathleen Baker-Gumprecht's experience as told in her article "Saved by a Psalm." While on her second solo flight in a hot-air balloon, Kathleen was in danger of plummeting to her death. She recounted, "Into my mind rushed the words of a psalm I had learned as a child: 'Call upon Me in the day of trouble: I will deliver thee' (Psalm 50:15).... I seized the verse as a drowning person clutches a rope." Kathleen felt God's presence and obeyed an urge to work the burner on the balloon, a step that made no sense at all. But this action saved her life.

Some psalms we can pray from memory because we've learned them by osmosis, having read or heard them countless times. If you would like to commit a more extensive supply to memory and make it more likely that you go about with a song in your heart, here are some tips:

❖ Reflect on the meaning of the verse. Look up unfamiliar words in a dictionary.
❖ Repeat the verse aloud often.
❖ Write the verse several times.
❖ Display the verse where you will see it: on your desk, dresser, or refrigerator.
❖ Make up motions to do as you say the verse.

♪ psalm notes...

On awaking each morning, you might pray, "This is the day that the LORD has made; let us be rejoice and be glad in it" (Psalm 118:24). On retiring you might pray, "I will both lie down and sleep in peace; for you alone, O LORD, make me lie down in safety" (Psalm 4:8).

Psalms were originally written on papyrus, made from the stem of the papyrus, a reed in the Nile Delta in Egypt. The stem was stripped, and the sticky pith inside was sliced into strips. These were laid next to each other, and another layer was laid horizontally across them. The strips were then pounded together and dried. A round object like a shell was used to smooth the papyrus. The scrolls were usually kept in clay jars for protection and sometimes sealed.

❖ Sing the verse to a tune.
❖ If the verse if long, break it down and memorize one section at a time.
❖ Work on memorizing a verse right before you go to bed. (For some reason, it stays in the mind better.)
❖ Memorize verses while traveling, exercising, jogging, or waiting in a doctor's office.
❖ Set memorization goals for yourself.
❖ Be accountable to another person in your memorization work. Perhaps you can learn the psalms together.

# Lectio Divina
# with the Psalms

*"How sweet are your words to my taste,*
*sweeter than honey to my mouth!"*
Psalm 119:103

*ectio divina* (Latin for "sacred reading) is making a comeback. It is a form of prayer that originated with the Hebrews. They would memorize and meditate on the word of God until it became part of them. In Christian tradition, lectio divina flourished in monasteries when not everyone owned a personal copy of the Bible. Monks would take a word from Scripture and ruminate on it. The ultimate aim of this prayer was to be united with God. Wilfrid Stinissen, a Swedish Carmelite, describes this power of the word in modern terminology: "As a rocket fires off a spaceship outside the earth into space, so the word can propel us into God's endlessness."

You don't have to be a monk or a professional contemplative to pray lectio divina. It is for anyone destined to live forever with God—that's every person, including you.

## How to Do It

To begin lectio divina, sit quietly and think about what you are about to do. You might become aware of your body, your breathing, and the sounds around you. You might listen to soft music. Ask the help of the Holy Spirit. Realize that God is present, looking at you and loving you.

Lectio divina has four steps, which have been compared to rungs on

Saint Teresa of Avila said, "We have such a great God that a single one of his words contain thousands of secrets."

Jacob's ladder. (In Genesis 28:10-17, the patriarch Jacob dreams of a ladder that reached to heaven. Angels were ascending and descending, and the Lord was beside him.) The four steps take you to God dwelling in your heart:

❖ *Lectio* (reading). Read the passage slowly, pausing now and then to allow the words to enter you. The purpose of this focused reading is to awaken your heart to prayer, not to stimulate your mind to curiosity. Suddenly a word or phrase will choose you. It will stand out, and you will resonate with it. Let the word or phrase touch you. Repeat the words that snagged your mind and let them sink into your heart. Savor the words, and let them saturate you and form your heart. This step is like putting the reading into your mouth—as a grape is placed in a winepress. As you say the words, you will wonder why they have attracted your attention and what this might mean for you. This moves you into the next step.

❖ *Meditatio* (meditating). Now wrestle with the words, probe them, ponder them, and seek their meaning for your life and your unique relationship with God. Ask God, "What are you saying to me?" Let the fullness of the words penetrate you. You need not keep repeating the word or phrase. Just concentrate on the essence of its meaning. Let it become part of you. This step is comparable to pressing a grape, drawing the juice that will ferment into wine. Remember that vintage wine takes time. At some point you will realize the meaning the word or phrase has for you. This is the "aha moment." You are moved deeply by God's Word and are ready to respond, to enter the third step.

❖ *Oratio* (praying). In this step your prayer moves from mind to heart. Talk to God spontaneously about the word or phrase in intimate conversation. Let your heart speak, sing, celebrate, or cry. What response do the words call forth from you—praise? thanksgiving? sorrow? peace? commitment? enthusiasm? conviction? Stay with those feelings. Don't try to understand them. Just remain in loving silence, letting yourself desire God and letting God desire you. Try to put yourself at the disposal of God's Spirit, preparing yourself for God's action. Your mind and heart should be focused on God. When you feel it is time to return to the reading, do so. It could be, though, that this step catapults you into the final, climactic step of lectio divina, which is contemplation.

❖ *Contemplatio* (contemplation). Contemplation is "a simple loving gaze." Be alone with God in the great silence that is too deep for words. Here God takes over your faculties and assumes the lead. You have a direct experience of God. Listen to what God says to you. Enjoy what is happening. The goal of lectio divina is this last step, union with God. During this step, it may seem as though nothing is happening, as you are simply resting in God's embrace. There may be no perceptible union. This is deceptive. A piece of Zen wisdom sheds light on this situation: "Sitting still/doing nothing, Spring comes/and the grass grows by itself." Saint John of the Cross, a 16th-century mystic, once said, "Silence is God's first language."

Notice that the first three steps of lectio divina involve doing, and the last step is simply being. The first three steps move from words to the fourth step, which is wordlessness. These four steps, however, can occur in any order and last any length of time. You may repeat a step several times or just do one

♪ psalm notes...

The rock band U2's song "*40*," which was their concert closer for years, is based on Psalm 40:1–3. It is one of their fifteen most frequently performed songs.

During the Eucharist, at Communion time the early Church always prayed Psalm 34:8 "O taste and see that the LORD is good."

step. When you are distracted or can't sustain your prayer, return to the Scripture passage and read it again until another word or phrase strikes you. It is recommended that you share your experiences with lectio divina with a person you love and trust, both to keep yourself honest about what you are experiencing and to allow what is happening to you to overflow into another person.

## An Illustration

Let's say you have chosen Psalm 139 for lectio divina:

❖ (Step one) You read the psalm until you come to the words, "You knit me together in my mother's womb." Those words captivate you somehow.

❖ (Step two) You begin to meditate on the line. You ponder the ingenuity of God, who devised such a mind-boggling way to reproduce us. You reflect on the various parts, powers, and talents that comprise you. You think about the woman who gave you birth. Suddenly you come to the realization that God loves you like a mother, even more than your mother loves you.

❖ (Step three) This thought moves you to prayer. You express heartfelt thanks to God for loving you: "O God, your tender love for me is unexplainable. You are so great, and I, more than anyone, know how undeserving I am of your attention and care. Thank you for your goodness and love." As you pray, a strong desire to love God in return may come over you.

❖ (Step four) You may be swept up into a sacred experience where God and you simply enjoy each other's presence and love.

## Expanding the Concept

Someone has renamed the steps as these four movements:

* receiving (lectio)
* appropriating (meditatio)
* responding (oratio)
* union (contemplatio).

John of the Cross listed the four steps this way:
*See in* reading
*and you will find in* meditation.
*Know in* prayer
*and it will be opened to you in* contemplation.

Dom Marmion paraphrased the steps poetically:
*We read*
*under the eye of God*
*until the heart is touched*
*and leaps to flame.*

These steps have also been compared to stages in a relationship. Lectio is like getting acquainted. When we first meet someone, it is usual formal and the focus is on exchanging information. Meditatio is like friendliness. As we get to know someone, we engage in conversation that is more informal. Oratio is like the higher level of a relationship, that is, friendship which involves faithfulness and commitment. Finally, contemplatio is comparable to moving toward union, a relationship characterized by intimacy and surrender.

The four steps have also been matched to the senses of Scripture. In lectio we primarily operate on the level of the literal sense, merely soaking in the words as they appear. During meditatio we work with the allegorical sense of the words, delving into their deeper meanings. The oratio stage is

♪ psalm notes...

Early Irish Celtic monks prayed all 150 psalms within each twenty-four-hour period.

♪ psalm
notes...

Psalm 121 is called "the psalm of the keeper" or "the psalm of the helper" because in a few lovely images it captures God's provident care for us.

comparable to the moral sense, for in this stage we let the reading touch our lives as we pray and respond. Finally, contemplatio is like the eschatological sense, when we focus on our supernatural existence; for in this stage we have a foretaste of eternity where we are one with God.

## The Fifth Step

Some people add a fifth step to lectio divina: *operatio* (action). Our prayer should enflame and energize us to take action in our lives. Then we will be one of those whom Jesus praised when he proclaimed, "Blessed rather are those who hear the word of God and obey it" (Luke 11:28).

Over time, lectio divina results in self-knowledge, inner freedom, compassion for self and others, and more concern for the global community. It forms in you a listening heart so that you become more reflective, more attuned to God in everyday events. You may also realize that you experience an increase of the fruits of the Holy Spirit: love, joy, peace, patience, generosity, faithfulness, kindness, gentleness, self-control, and purity.

### *In Chorus*

Lection divina may be carried out in a group. Form groups of no more than four or five. Light a candle to recall God's presence. Guide each group through this process:

❖ In each group one person reads a passage while all listen.

❖ Another person reads the same passage. People read with different intonations and expressions, uncovering different meanings.

❖ Allow quiet time for a word or phrase to touch everyone's heart.

❖ Invite the participants to reflect aloud. (Reflecting differs from discussion. In this step, let each person share his or her thoughts without any response from others.) Some may simply share a word or phrase that has meaning for them.

❖ Play a related song.

❖ Invite the participants to make a prayer response aloud, one or two simple sentences that their reflection prompts them to pray. This can be a prayer of thanksgiving, petition, adoration, love, or sorrow. (You may need to give an example or two. Tell the pray-ers that it's all right if their prayer is the same as someone else's.)

❖ Sit in silence for a considerable time.

# The Liturgy of the Hours
# A Divine Work

*"O magnify the LORD with me,*
*and let us exalt his name together."*
Psalm 34:3

You are probably aware that cloistered nuns and monks silently gather in chapel at midnight and other hours of the day and night to pray. What you might not know is that they are praying the Liturgy of the Hours, or Prayer of Christians, that originally was a prayer of the laity. Every day the Church prays psalms in this, her official prayer, which is also called the Divine Office (meaning "holy work"). Priests (using a breviary) and religious men and women have prayed this prayer for centuries. Today a growing number of laypeople are reclaiming this prayer and discovering that it bolsters and enriches their spiritual lives. Some parishes pray its Morning Prayer on the Easter Triduum: Holy Thursday, Good Friday, and Holy Saturday. Other parishes pray Morning or Evening Prayer several days a week or for special occasions. Through the Divine Office, the Church makes Earth a planet of continuous praise as Christians all over the globe pray twenty-four hours a day.

## Historical Development

The Prayer of Christians has its roots in Hebrew prayer. Psalm 119:164 mentions praying seven times a day and also praying at midnight. The early Christians followed this practice, praying the psalms and reading from the Old Testament, gradually adding their own prayers and reading from their

Historically the rosary developed from the psalms and was referred to as "the breviary on beads." The many illiterate people, who could not read the psalms, began praying 150 Our Fathers (paternosters) on beads as a substitute. This evolved into praying the 150 Hail Marys in sets of fifty, each fifty devoted to meditating on a group of mysteries: Joyful, Sorrowful, and Glorious. Each decade concluded with a Glory Be, the prayer that is prayed at the end of a psalm. With Pope John Paul II's addition of the Luminous mysteries, the complete rosary now has 200 Hail Marys.

own Scriptures. The Acts of the Apostles mentions specific hours for prayer: for example, Peter went to the roof to pray about the sixth hour (Acts 10:9); Peter and John were going to the Temple at the hour of prayer, the ninth hour (Acts 3:1); and about midnight Paul and Silas were praying and singing hymns (Acts 16:25).

At first Christian prayer was held in the morning and evening. Today these two hours are known as the *hinge hours*, on which the whole cycle of hours depend. Some think that the first part of the Eucharist, the Liturgy of the Word, was conducted even when the Eucharist wasn't celebrated, and this practice evolved into the Divine Office. Just like the Mass, the Liturgy of the Hours has special prayers for the seasons of the liturgical year, for feast days, and for Mary and the saints.

By the end of the fifth century, this psalm-centered prayer was fairly well set so that the whole day would be sanctified. The hours were *matins* at midnight, *lauds* at dawn, *prime* in the morning, *terce* in midmorning, *sext* at noon, *none* in midafternoon, *vespers* (evening prayer), and *compline* (night prayer). Today matins is replaced by the Office of Readings and can be prayed anytime. Prime has been abolished to align the Office with the biblical number seven, the number signifying perfection, based on the seven-day account of creation in Genesis. The seven prayer times are also consistent with the Israelite tradition.

The hours of the Divine Office coincide with key events in the Church's life as follows: Morning Prayer (the Resurrection), Midmorning Prayer (Pentecost), Noon (crucifixion and the realization that Gentiles should be accepted in the Church), Midday Prayer (death of Jesus), and Evening Prayer (the Last Supper).

The office is prayed by both eastern and western

monks. In the sixth century Saint Benedict, the father of Western monasticism, called the office *Opus Dei*, "The Work of God," and considered it the monk's supreme occupation. Benedict worked out a scheme whereby his monks would pray all 150 psalms over the course of a week. In today's Divine Office, each hour has three psalms, except for Morning and Evening Prayer, which have two psalms and another canticle from Scripture. All of the psalms are prayed over the course of a month.

## The Structure of the Hours

The Divine Office has been called "the psalms in a frame." Each hour (except the first, which begins with an invitatory) opens with the psalm verse "O God, come to my assistance. O LORD, make haste to help me" (Psalm 70:1). The usual invitatory that opens the first hour of the office is Psalm 95, which begins "O come, let us sing to the LORD." This psalm contains "O that today you would listen to his voice!" (verse 7), which is a fitting plea for the start of the day. The basic format for each hour is:

❖ A hymn
❖ Three psalms (or two psalms and a canticle) with antiphons before and after, each followed by a psalm-prayer that "collects" the main ideas of the psalm
❖ A reading from Scripture
❖ A short versicle (part of a verse) and response
❖ A canticle (Lauds includes the *Magnificat*, Evening Prayer the *Benedictus*, and Night Prayer the *Nunc Dimittus*.)
❖ Intercessions
❖ The Our Father
❖ Closing Prayer (Night Prayer concludes with a Marian antiphon, such as the Hail Mary, Hail, Holy Queen, or *Regina Caeli*.)

♪ psalm notes...

Saint Basil the Great, the fourth-century founder of Eastern monasticism, said, "If the ocean is beautiful and worthy of praise to God, how much more beautiful is the conduct of this Christian assembly, where the voices of men, women, and children, blended and sonorous like the waves that break upon the beach, rise amidst our prayers to the very presence of God!"

Saint Francis of Assisi
produced his own
Office of the Passion
for the Franciscans,
which, despite the
title, actually covered
all the mysteries of
Jesus' life. For this
office he composed
fifteen original psalms
that are mostly psalm
verses from Scripture
carefully laced
together.

## Praying the Divine Office

You might purchase a book of Christian Prayer and pray one or more of the hours each day yourself. Or you can locate a religious community or parish near you that prays the Divine Office together and join them for prayer. On the Internet, too, you can participate in the Office, what Quaker mystic Thomas Kelly called "the great orbit of prayer." At www.universalis.com you will find the entire Prayer of Christians for each day. Or if you prefer, you can also pray just the psalms daily with monks by going to www.blueclouds.org and clicking on "Psalms."

The Church's "General Instruction of the Liturgy of the Hours" of 1971 encourages laity to celebrate part of the Liturgy of the Hours. It suggests that families, known as the domestic Church, pray parts of it sometimes in order to enter more deeply into the life of the Church. This document can be found on the Internet at www.catholicliturgy.com under "Documents."

# Glossary of Hebrew Concepts

Knowing about the worldview and the culture of the Israelites helps in understanding the psalms. Naturally their concepts differ from ours some two thousand years later. Some of their thinking is explained here.

**ark of the covenant:** This cabinet, constructed by Moses at God's direction during the Exodus, contained the tablets of the ten commandments. To the Hebrews it was a sign of God's presence. Later David had it brought to Jerusalem where it was kept in the Holy of Holies in the Temple. When the Babylonians destroyed Jerusalem in 576 B.C., the ark disappeared. In the psalms, the ark of the covenant is often referred to as the footstool of God.

**covenant**: The promises that bound the Hebrews to God suffused their whole life. They were to keep God's law and God, they knew, would be faithful in being their loving and saving God.

**fear of the Lord**: Fear of God meant having awe and profound reverence for God. It did not mean being afraid of God.

**fool**: A fool was not a silly or unintelligent person but someone who did not follow God's law, who made a mistake.

**God**: The Israelites' concept of there being only one God evolved. At first they thought their God was first among many, "a great King above all gods" (Psalm 95:3), so some earlier psalms refer to other gods. Nevertheless, their God was unique in that he called forth love from them and a longing to be with him—a relationship that was unthinkable for pagans and their gods. Gradually the Israelites came to know their God as one true God, the God who created the universe and brought them salvation.

Psalm 45 is unique in that it is a psalm written for the wedding of an Israelite king.

**heart**: To the Israelites the heart was the center of a person's whole being and action: physically, intellectually, emotionally, psychologically, and spiritually. Because they believed a person's life depended on God's breath *(ruah)*, that word is sometimes translated as heart.

**Jerusalem** (also called Zion and holy mountain): To the Hebrews, their holy city was extremely precious, the navel of the world and their true home. We Christians have nothing to compare to it. It was David's city, which he won by capturing a fortress there from the Jebusites. Jerusalem became the capital city of Israel and the site of the ark of the covenant and the Temple, making it the place where God was present. When Jerusalem was destroyed, all was lost. The name Jerusalem means "city of peace" from the word *shalom*. The city's original name was simply Salem.

**king**: Israel was a theocracy in which, as in other ancient countries, there was no separation of church and state. To the Hebrews, their king was "the anointed one," a "son of God." The king spoke for God and was to be reverenced and obeyed. Not merely a secular leader, the king presided at liturgies and offered sacrifice.

**Law**: The law of God contained in the Torah (teaching), the first five books of the Bible, was viewed as a gift. It taught the Israelites what God called them to do and become. Following this law led to a good, joyful existence. The law was a reason to praise and thank God.

**name of God**: God's name was synonymous with God's self and carried God's power. The Hebrews were in such awe of this name that they never said it. The personal name of God revealed to Moses was the tetragrammaton *YHWH*, which becomes *Yahweh* when vowels are added in English. The Jews substituted the word *Adonai*, or Lord, for this name. The term *Elohim* was a general name for any god or gods.

**retribution**: The Hebrews thought that eventually God would reward the good and punish the wicked on earth. When they realized that the wicked sometimes enjoyed a good life, this strained their faith. Nevertheless they continued to hope in God and believe in his ultimate justice.

**Sheol** (the pit, netherworld, the underworld, Hades): This was the terrible Abode of the Dead, a common grave in the depths of the earth, also called the land of forgetfulness. The concept of an afterlife in Hebrew thought surfaced slightly before the first century. Until then, the Hebrews thought that only God was immortal. All of the dead, good and bad, led a silent, shadowy, uncomfortable existence in Sheol. Although it was not hell, a place of punishment, Sheol was a place where one no longer experienced God's presence. Because of this concept of Sheol, the Hebrews had a high regard for a long life on earth. Sheol is also used as a metaphor for a distressing situation, comparable to our use of the word *hell*.

**soul**: Thinking of a human being as having two parts, a body and a soul, was foreign to the Hebrews. Where a psalm mentions "soul," think of it as referring to the whole mystery of a person's being. In translations "soul" has sometimes been used as a synonym for "life."

**Temple**: The Temple was in Jerusalem and was the central place of worship and the only place where sacrifices were made. It was God's palace and had an outer court called the Court of the Gentiles, the Woman's Court, and the Court of Men. Inside was the Holy of Holies where God was present. No one was permitted to enter that room except for the high priest once a year on Yom Kippur to offer incense and sprinkle the blood of sacrifice.

♪ psalm notes...

Saint Ambrose said, "Although all Scripture breathes the grace of God, yet sweet beyond all others is the Book of Psalms. History instructs, the Law teaches, Prophecy announces, rebukes, chastens, Morality persuades; but in the Book of Psalms we have the fruit of all these, and a kind of medicine for the salvation of men."

With its images of creation, weather, and bountiful crops, Psalm 65 makes a wonderful Thanksgiving psalm.

**water**: On one hand the Hebrews, a desert people, valued water as a precious, life-giving commodity. On the other hand, influenced by Babylonian mythology, they viewed water as evil, a place where sea monsters like Rahab and Leviathan lurked. God however, who brings forth life out of the watery chaos in the book of Genesis, continues to subdue and command the waters above, around, and below the earth.

**world**: The Hebrews, like their neighbors, thought that the earth was set on pillars and surrounded by water. Below the earth was water. The sky was a curved bowl with gates that opened to let in the waters above the earth.

**Zion**: This was another word for Jerusalem. It is also personified as daughter Zion in the Scriptures.

# Annotated Bibliography

## Bibles

*New American Bible*: This is the official Catholic Bible for the United States. Has introductions and footnotes. Most widely used among Catholics in the United States because it is used in the liturgy. Latest editions contain a 1991 revision of the Book of Psalms.

*New Jerusalem Bible*: A translation of a French Bible with scholarly and theological footnotes. Popular among Catholics.

*New Revised Standard Version Bible*: Approved for use by both Catholics and Protestants. Has more inclusive language.

## Versions of the Psalms

*Children's Psalms to Pray, Sing, and Do*. David Haas and Brent Beck, Cincinnati, OH: Saint Anthony Messenger Press, 2004. Forty-eight psalms translated for children from four to eight years of age.

*The Message: Psalms*: Eugene H. Peterson, Colorado Springs, CO: Navpress Publishing Group, 2004. A wonderful paraphrase for contemporary people that makes you look at the psalms in a fresh way.

*Prayers Before an Awesome God: The Psalms for Teenagers*: David Haas, Winona, MN: Saint Mary Press, 2000. Teen-friendly versions of the psalms with ideas and indexes for their use.

*Psalms*: The Saint John Bible series. Donald Jackson, Artistic Director and Illuminator, Collegeville, MN: The Liturgical Press, 2006. Hand-lettered psalms are accompanied by striking illustrations. Every page features a gold image that graphically renders the chanting of the monks from Saint John's

St. Teresa of Avila
died praying over and
over, "A sacrifice to
God is an afflicted
spirit. A humble and
contrite heart O God,
thou wilt not despise."
(Psalm 51:17)

Abbey as a reminder that the psalms are sacred songs. Colors represent different themes and designs symbolize the different types of psalms.

*Psalms Now*: Leslie Brandt, Saint Louis, MO: Concordia Publishing House, 1973. Informal paraphrases that interpret texts for the contemporary world.

*The Psalms*: Ronald Knox, New York: Sheed & Ward, 1955. A translation from the New Latin version of the Psalms, with reference to the Hebrew.

*Psalms Anew*: Maureen Leach and Nancy Schreck, Winona, MN: Saint Mary's Press, 1986. Psalms using inclusive language. The book has tables of psalms for the four-week cycle of Liturgy of the Hours.

*Psalms for Praying: An Invitation to Wholeness*: Nan C. Merrill, New York: Continuum International Publishing Group, 2006 (anniversary edition). This poetic version of the psalms is gentle, nonviolent, and lovely. Contemporary language makes the verses more meaningful. For instance the chaff that the wind drives away in Psalm 1:4 is converted to "dandelions."

*The Psalms in Other Words*: Hubert van Zeller, Springfield, IL: Templegate, 1964. Readable paraphrases of the psalms.

### Books about the Psalms

*The Book of Psalms*: Toni Craven, Collegeville, MN: The Liturgical Press. A Michael Glazier Book, 1992. Message of Spirituality series. Beliefs, attitudes, and practices of prayer implied in the psalms about those who prayed them.

*Bread in the Wilderness*: Thomas Merton, O.C.S.O., New York: New Directions Publishing Corporation, 1953 (1997 reprint). A classic on the psalms. Merton beautifully presents the psalms as manna in the desert, daily nourishment, not only for monks but for all Christians.

*Learning to Pray Through the Psalms*: James W. Sire, Downers Grove, IL: Intervarsity Press, 2006. Ten chapters, each on a psalm and how to pray it; small-group study instructions

*Light in the Darkness: New Reflections on the Psalms for Every Day of the Year*: Joan D. Chittester, New York: Crossroad Publishing, 1998. This popular author provides a brief reflection on a psalm for every day during the year.

*The Message of the Psalms: A Theological Commentary*: Walter Brueggemann, Augsburg, MN, 1984. Brueggemann explains the pattern of orientation, disorientation, and reorientation that he found in the psalms.

*Praying the Psalms*: Thomas Merton, O.C.S.O., Collegeville, MN: The Liturgical Press, 1956. Shows how to draw out the richness of worship from the Psalter and to use it to achieve "the peace that comes from submission to God's will and from perfect confidence in Him."

*Reflections on the Psalms*: C.S. Lewis, New York: Harcourt, Brace Jovanovich, 1958. Thoughts the author had while reading the psalms, including problems he faced and lights he experienced.

*A Short Dictionary of the Psalms*: Jean-Pierre Prevost and Mary M. Misrahi, Collegeville, MN: The Liturgical Press, 2003. Explanations of the significance of forty key words that are essential vocabulary of the psalms.

*What Am I That You Care for Me? Praying with the Psalms*: Carlo Maria Martine, Collegeville, MN: The Liturgical Press, 1988. An exploration of the themes of the psalms as useful for prayer.

♪ psalm notes...

Charles Spurgeon, a Protestant known as the Prince of Preachers, taught, "More and more is the conviction forced upon my heart that every man must traverse the territory of the Psalms himself if he would know what a goodly land they are. They flow with milk and honey, but not to strangers; they are only fertile to lovers of their hills and vales. None but the Holy Spirit can give a man the key to the Treasury of David; and even he gives it rather to experience than to study. Happy he who for himself knows the secret of the Psalms."

Like music that stirs the emotions, the psalms leave no heartstrings unplucked. For centuries they have moved people, and people have prayed them to move God.

## Commentaries/Reflections on the Psalms

*Berit Olam: Psalms*: Konrad Schaefer, O.S.B., Collegeville, MN: The Liturgical Press, 2001. Relates the poetic elements of the psalms, their historical context and traditional use in the liturgy and, most importantly, their value as a springboard to prayer.

*Out of the Depths: The Psalms Speak for Us Today*: Bernard W. Anderson, Philadelphia: The Westminster Press, 1995 (revised edition). An excellent guide for the study of the psalms written by a seminary professor.

*Prayerbook of the King: The Psalms*: Charles Dollen, New York: Alba House, 1998. Musings on each psalm, jam-packed with quotations from the spiritual writers of the ages.

*Praying the Psalms with Saint Padre Pio*: Eileen Dunn Bertanzetti, Huntington, IN: Our Sunday Visitor, 2006. Pairs each psalm with Padre Pio's writings, which give insight into the psalm.

*The Psalms Are Yours*: Roland E. Murphy, O. Carm., Mahwah, NJ: Paulist Press, 1993. An introduction to the psalms and a commentary on them that is easy to understand.

*Psalms for Contemplation*: Carlos G. Valles, S.J., Chicago, IL: Loyola Press, 1990. Personal reflections in the form of a prayer on each psalm.

*The Psalms for Today: Praying an Old Book in a New Way*: Mark Link, S.J., Calencia, CA: Tabor Publishing, 1988. Brief thoughts on key verses from each of the psalms with questions for reflection.

*Psalms I and Psalms II*. Carroll Stuhlmueller, Wilmington, DE: Michael Glazier, Inc., 1983. Commentary by a renowned scripture scholar.

*A Turbulent Peace: The Psalms for Our Time*: Ray Waddle, Nashville, TN: Upper Room Books, 2004. A one-page meditation for each psalm, combining observations about current religious trends and

Bible history with personal stirrings of the spirit.

*With a Listening Heart: Biblical and Spiritual Reflections on the Psalms*: Bertrand A. Buby, S.M., New York: Alba House, 2005. Succinctly points out for each psalm what to look for to derive maximum benefit and offers the author's prayerful reflections on the text.

## Other Books

*Nourished by the Word: Reading the Bible Contemplatively*: Wilfrid Stinissen, Liguori, MO: Liguori, 1999. Puts the reader into deep spiritual waters regarding what the Bible is and whom it contains.

*Praying the Sunday Psalms*: Michael Goonan, S.S.P., New York: Alba House, 2001. Reflects on the riches of the psalm verses set down for each of the Sundays of the three cycles (A, B, and C) and considers the other readings in the light of the psalm.

*A Retreat with the Psalms: Resources for Personal and Communal Prayer*: John C. Endres and Elizabeth Liebert, Mahwah, NJ: Paulist Press, 2001. Views the psalms as work of piety and art in a way that addresses the needs of a world seeking to counter injustice by a global peace born of personal peace through prayer and practice.

*Sacred Reading: The Ancient Art of Lectio Divina*: Casey Michael, Liguori, MO: Liguori, 1996. Leads the reader to a deeper sense of the real presence of God in Scripture, then shows how the fruits of lectio divina can be extended into a more contemplative lifestyle.

*Too Deep for Words: Rediscovering Lectio Divina*: Thelma Hall, Mahwah, NJ: Paulist Press, 1988. Offers 500 well-chosen Scripture texts for lectio divina, grouped by topic. A welcome aid for those just beginning scriptural prayer.

♪ psalm notes...

The fourth-century bishop St. Athanasius reportedly declared that "the Psalms have a unique place in the Bible because most of the Scripture speaks *to* us, while the Psalms speak *for* us."